More Praise for *Entrepreneurs in Every Generation*

"It was very hard for me to put the book down. Growi___ ____ ___ ___ _____ family, so much rings so true. I wonder had I read ___ _____ ___ ___ ___ ___ ___ might have been different. The book documents so much of what our family is living through! It has lots of great ideas for preparing the next generation to continue their roles as stewards of the brands and family participants."
   —William S. Fisher, Board Member, Gap Inc.

"Allan Cohen and Dita Sharma have written a highly insightful, clear, and pragmatic argument that innovation in family companies is essential for multi-generational success. This will help families understand how to innovate in every generation and how to develop leaders who can bring about needed change in the family business."
   —John Davis, Chair, Families in Business Program, Harvard Business School, and
   Chairman, Cambridge Advisors to Family Enterprise

"The entrepreneurial spirit in my family and our business has been one of the most important factors in our continued success through six generations. Finally, a book that not only acknowledges the importance of entrepreneurship to the long-term success of family businesses but also provides a practical guide to families who want to keep that entrepreneurial spark alive from generation to generation. This book is a joy to read and will transform the way you think about families in business."
   —Sylvia Shepard, former Chair and Founder, Smith Family Council, Menasha
   Corporation, fifth generation

"This is the clearest and most comprehensive list I have ever come across of all the key practices necessary to ensure the development of the entrepreneurial spirit in every generation. This 'Magna Carta' of transgenerational entrepreneur-ship should be made compulsory reading for all members of family businesses. This is the best gift I could have wished for! The authors cover all the issues I wrestled with over the past twenty-five years, as well as some I have not faced or seen yet but will now be prepared to handle. It is also very timely, as my older son is now less than two years away from entering university, and this book will be perfect for discussions between him and me."
   —Cyril Camus, fifth-generation owner and CEO, House of CAMUS Cognac

"I am so excited to see that finally a book has been written on entrepreneurship through generations. Entrepreneurship is generally abundant in the founder, and somehow the desire to do something different starts to fade away with the next generations. In my family I encourage and support entrepreneurship for the next generation."
   —Surya Jhunjhnuwala, founder and Managing Director, Naumi Hotels, Singapore

"Cohen and Sharma adopt a distinctive structure that advances the discussion of entrepreneurial issues in families and includes chapters that describe what to do and how to go about doing it. The text is inspired by research evidence and introduces key concepts that are illuminated by some recognizable family business cases drawn from many countries. The research does not clutter the presentation but rather highlights the intellectual origins of the ideas described."

—Ken Moores, former President, Bond University, and Consultant and Executive Chairman, Moores Family Enterprise, Australia

"*Entrepreneurs in Every Generation* is an inspiring read. Not only do the authors beautifully tie in the important role entrepreneurship plays in the sustainability of family enterprises, but they also provide real case studies and tools for change. A must-read for business owners and their families."

—Ramia M. El Agamy, Editor-in-Chief, *Tharawat* magazine, Dubai and Switzerland

"This new book by two well-respected academics in the family business field integrates insights from psychology, strategy, and change management with case studies from family companies around the world. An interesting and readable book that is especially useful for next generation family business members."

—Judy Green, PhD, President, Family Firm Institute

"Cohen and Sharma shed light on the key points needed to ignite the entrepreneurial spark within generations. They bundle this up in a beautiful and interactive way. A great read!"

—Willy Lin, Managing Director, Milo's Knitwear and Milo's Manufacturing, Hong Kong, second generation

"A great book for business families that are looking for a learning opportunity to build their business entrepreneurially. Flexibility and change are the essence of entrepreneurship in a rapidly transforming society such as India and other emerging market economies. Professors Allan Cohen and Pramodita Sharma, two stalwarts with several decades of accumulated combined wisdom in different countries, have brought together their insights on family entrepreneurship in this book. They have done an exceptionally good job of describing the 'what' and 'how' of building entrepreneurial family businesses. Their present contribution has the potential to be a change agent and create the road map for business families to be not only agents of transformation but also institution builders of the nation."

—Kavil Ramachandran, Executive Director, Thomas Schmidheiny Centre for Family Enterprise, Indian School of Business

ENTREPRENEURS
— *in Every* —
GENERATION

ENTREPRENEURS
— *in Every* —
GENERATION

How Successful Family Businesses

Develop Their Next Leaders

Allan R. Cohen and Pramodita Sharma

Berrett–Koehler Publishers, Inc.
a BK Business book

Berrett-Koehler Publishers, Inc.
1333 Broadway, Suite 1000
Oakland, CA 94612-1921
Tel: (510) 817-2277 Fax: (510) 817-2278 www.bkconnection.com

Ordering Information
Quantity sales. Special discounts are available on quantity purchases by corporations, associations, and others. For details, contact the "Special Sales Department" at the Berrett-Koehler address above.
Individual sales. Berrett-Koehler publications are available through most bookstores. They can also be ordered directly from Berrett-Koehler: Tel: (800) 929-2929; Fax: (802) 864-7626; www.bkconnection.com
Orders for college textbook/course adoption use. Please contact Berrett-Koehler: Tel: (800) 929-2929; Fax: (802) 864-7626.
Orders by U.S. trade bookstores and wholesalers. Please contact Ingram Publisher Services, Tel: (800) 509-4887; Fax: (800) 838-1149; E-mail: customer.service@ingrampublisherservices.com; or visit www.ingrampublisherservices.com/Ordering for details about electronic ordering.

Berrett-Koehler and the BK logo are registered trademarks of Berrett-Koehler Publishers, Inc.

Printed in the United States of America

Berrett-Koehler books are printed on long-lasting acid-free paper. When it is available, we choose paper that has been manufactured by environmentally responsible processes. These may include using trees grown in sustainable forests, incorporating recycled paper, minimizing chlorine in bleaching, or recycling the energy produced at the paper mill.

Library of Congress Cataloging-in-Publication Data

Names: Cohen, Allan R., author. | Sharma, Pramodita, author.
Title: Entrepreneurs in every generation : how successful family businesses
 develop their next leaders / Allan R Cohen and Pramodita Sharma.
Description: First Edition. | Oakland : Berrett-Koehler Publishers, Inc.,
 2016. | ?2015 | Includes bibliographical references.
Identifiers: LCCN 2015047989 | ISBN 9781626561663 (pbk.)
Subjects: LCSH: Family-owned business enterprises. | Leadership. |
 Entrepreneurship.
Classification: LCC HD62.25 .C64 2016 | DDC 658.4/21--dc23
LC record available at http://lccn.loc.gov/2015047989

Jacket Design: Kirk DouPonce/DogEared Design
Book Production: Adept Content Solutions

To Our Enterprising Families:

Cohen, Shatsky

Dada, Joshi, Sharma

CONTENTS

FOREWORD

The field of family business is undergoing dramatic change. The definition of success now surpasses firm survival and continuity to include family success. The family business field also recognizes that family success and sustainability increasingly embrace other forms of collective family purpose—joint philanthropy, new businesses, family offices, family cohesion, learning, and fun.

While most all family business writings focus on the business and/or the family, *Entrepreneurs in Every Generation* shows readers how success is assuring next generation entrepreneurial leadership in three dimensions: the business, the owning family, and the organization that nurtures both. Applying the entrepreneurial mind-set to all three dimensions, authors Allan Cohen and Pramodita Sharma define the challenges and the role for leadership; applying the entrepreneurial mind-set in all three dimensions is what sets family enterprises apart.

This book captures fresh insights by going beyond best practices. Viewed through the diverse lenses of the authors themselves, cases from all over the world are exciting to study and compelling to replicate. But the book goes further. In each dimension it not only reviews best practices, but it also urges special attention to the uniqueness of context. Even further, it guides the reader through helpful work sheets on how to understand and adapt to context.

By examining how evolving and improving organizational practices fuel sustainability, the book's lessons provide special insight into the art of continuity, providing actionable ideas on what successful entrepreneurs do and how they do it. By using the example of past generations to light the way for succeeding generations, next-generation entrepreneurial leaders can maximize the benefits of a family enterprise culture. The authors stimulate by highlighting many values that drive sustainability. Some of the values that stand out in their cases are

> stewardship;
> long-term thinking;
> attending to all stakeholders;
> innovation;
> adding value to customers;
> hunger for excellence;
> continuous improvement; and
> walking in the shoes of others.

These common values remind readers that there are many age-old truths to synthesize with the new insights for next generation entrepreneurs.

Perhaps the biggest challenge for family leaders is how to lead change in a densely developed and long-established organization and/or family system. To address this challenge, the authors introduce a powerful and succinct model for leading change—the "Iron Laws of Influence for Enterprising Families."

Pramodita Sharma and Allan Cohen are thought leaders in the new field of family enterprise, or enterprising families. *Entrepreneurs in Every Generation* champions growth—business growth, family growth, and organizational growth. Next-generation leaders have the talent to find the new ways to create that growth.

John L. Ward, Clinical Professor of Family Enterprises
Center for Family Enterprises
Kellogg School of Management
Chicago, USA

INTRODUCTION

In themselves, families are endlessly fascinating. They are the crucibles in which we learn to interact with and relate to those close and distant to us, to compete and love, and to make sense of the world. The basic assumptions governing families are derived from the emotional relationships in them.[1] A business, on the other hand, is task-oriented, created to produce a product or service that adds value for customers and owners alike. Its survival and longevity is determined by its financial performance over time. When overlapped as family business—all the complexities of making a living with all the dynamics of family membership—it is no wonder that there are so many variations, so many challenges, and so few one-dimensional, one-size-fits-all answers. But we can learn from others' experiences and research findings to develop tailored answers for our unique family and its enterprises.[2]

Enterprising families—in which each generation adds a layer of entrepreneurial contributions to the work of previous generations—are found in all regions of the world and in all facets of economy and society. The enterprises they run may be small, medium, or large. Their markets may be local or global. Their products may range from mundane, everyday items or services to the most technologically advanced ones. But what all have in common is that somehow they learn to

Enterprising families—in which each generation adds a layer of entrepreneurial contributions to the work of previous generations—are found in all regions of the world and in all facets of economy and society.

navigate the fine line between family and business to be successful on both family and business dimensions simultaneously.

It certainly isn't automatic or easy to instill in the next generation the necessary hunger and talent to find new and better ways to do things, find and service customers, finance the enterprise, and lead for the future. All are needed to create families and organizations that generate the new ideas, practices, products, and passion that cross generations. Our personal involvement with family business has led us to address enterprising families at all stages of their careers. We will use many examples of successful family firms around the world that have done and currently are doing what it takes to improve the odds that their enterprises can continue successfully into the future.

How Some Family Companies Innovate

Here are a few examples of the family companies that have innovated across generations and responded to changes in markets and business models.

Success against tough odds. How many text or email messages did you receive today? And, in comparison, how many letters came in an envelope? Most people now receive many more electronic communications than physical ones. If you are like us, perhaps you recall the delightful feeling of writing a letter to a loved one on special stationery or checking the mail box for days eagerly waiting to touch the envelope and the letter it carried. Or waiting anxiously for a payment to arrive in that special envelope with a clever plastic window that let the carrier read your name. Or the nervous wait for your grades to arrive in a distinctive envelope from the registrar's office. Email attachments and electronic drop boxes have taken over the task of moving X-rays, photographs, and tickets around. What happened to those family businesses that made the envelopes that once carried letters, checks, or other documents from one place to the next? Did they collapse over time under the weight of new technologies? Most did, but not all!

Tension Envelope Corporation[3] of Kansas City in the United States currently produces over 12 billion envelopes a year generating annual revenues in excess of 211 million dollars. A family-owned and -operated business in its fourth generation, this enterprise was founded by brothers William and Maurice Berkowitz in 1886. Despite the takeover of communications by computers and telephones, this company has enjoyed growth and stability for over 125 years, while others in its industry have perished under pressure. Their website declares that "it's an exciting time to be in business" while acknowledging the changes and challenges "posed by technological advances, environmental concerns, and postal regulations."

For many, words like *innovation* or *entrepreneurship* do not jump to mind when they think of a simple everyday product like an envelope. Think again. What are the different types of envelopes you have seen? In addition to the "Standard Commercial Envelopes," the "Envelope Gallery" of the Tension Corporation lists products like "Special Opener Envelopes," "Hot Note Envelopes," "Advanced 4-Color Flexo Envelopes," "Special Window Envelopes," "Hot Potato Envelopes," "2-Way Eco Envelopes," "Large Mailers," "CD/DVD Disk Sleeves & Bind-in's," "Send-n-Return Envelopes," "Packaging Envelopes," and "Seed Envelopes"—the list goes on to add different textures and embossing.

In addition to the seven envelope manufacturing plants at the core of this family business, Tension Corporation has grown beyond the borders of the United States and also added packaging and automation manufacturing to its portfolio. The entrepreneurial spirit seems to be imbued deeply in the culture of this company: over the years it has held more patents than any other envelope manufacturer in the country. Bill Berkley,[4] the fourth-generation president and CEO, notes that his "great-grandfather believed that innovation solves customers' issues, and [they] continue to apply for patents to continue this legacy."

Innovation over generations of family leadership has no geographic bounds. Caran d'Ache, a Swiss family enterprise, has been a leading manufacturer and supplier of pencils, fine-art materials, and luxury stationery throughout the world. Since its establishment in 1915, this company has relentlessly pursued technical excellence and innovation regardless of changes in the business environment. Carole Hübscher, chair of Caran d'Ache's Board of Directors, explains:

Our business has been through a lot. In the 1930s, for instance, it was difficult to get wood for our pencil production. We needed to find alternatives and we designed pencils with a metal body that are trademarked by Caran d'Ache as the 'clutch pencil.' We also tried to produce our pencils with fine Swiss woods which were hard to work with. It took us nearly seventy years to figure it out.[5]

Carol's father Jacques Hübscher is credited with diversifying the company's production, introducing luxury writing instruments and extending the company's presence to more than ninety countries. The current generation of leaders, while continuing to excel in quality products and process innovations, is simultaneously focused on staying at the leading edge of sustainable development and opening flagship Caran d'Ache stores that are aligned with the company's values.

In another part of the world, five generations of the Murugappa[6] family in India have innovated and diversified their business portfolio over the past 115 years. What started as a money-lending and banking business in Burma (now Myanmar) in 1900 diversified into rubber plantations, textiles, insurance, and stock brokerage in Ceylon (now Sri Lanka), Malaya, and Vietnam by 1915. With continuous expansion through acquisitions, joint ventures, new product launches, and green-field projects and with annual revenues of over a billion US dollars since 2003, the Murugappa Group of Companies is one of India's leading business conglomerates. It spans twenty-eight businesses, including nine listed companies in diverse industries such as abrasives, auto components, bio-products, plantations, and sugar, to name a few. While the family drives entrepreneurship, strategy, and governance, nonfamily executives lead the operations. Separation of ownership and management, with focus on the core values of *arthashastra*—the fundamental principle of economic activity that no one with whom the company transacts will lose—continues to guide this highly respected enterprising family of India.

Can you innovate if your industry is disappearing? Consider the transition of the Italian Falck Group; it dominated the iron and steel industry in Italy for almost seventy years from 1906 into the 1970s but suffered heavy losses in the 1980s and 1990s due to the structural industry crisis, only to re-emerge as a leader in renewable energy in the 2000s. This experience suggests enterprising families can accomplish this feat. The founding and evolution of the Falck Group has been well documented by the prominent economic historian Harold James in his 2006 book *Family Capitalism: Wendels, Haniels, Falcks, and the Continental European Model.* This case is remarkable because a visionary family member worked closely with a few savvy and astute nonfamily executives to ably redirect his family's focus and identity from the steel industry (with which its name had become synonymous) to build on the founder's entrepreneurial spirit and move the company from steel to the renewable energy industry.[7] For the most part, this turnaround was accomplished while keeping the family's solidarity intact. The younger brother of the turnaround family champion is today the chairman of Groupo Falck, as this company enjoys a Henokien position—an honor accorded only to fewer than fifty companies that are at least 200 years old and run by an heir of the founder, with the original family holding a majority stake or voting rights.

What makes some succeed? It is certainly not a new phenomenon for companies to innovate over generations of leaders and overcome not only industrial evolutions but also environmental or manmade disasters such as earthquakes, famines, wars, or accidents. Magazines such as *Fast Company* and *Forbes* release annual lists of the most innovative companies, and some of them, like General Electric and 3M, have been around for over a century. Countless books have been written both on innovation and the dilemmas of innovators or founding entrepreneurs, as well as on organizational leadership. What we explore is whether the mantras in these writings are equally effective for enterprises controlled by one or a few dominant families. With the complexities introduced by intermingling of kinship ties with the cutthroat realities of the business world, how do enterprising families like the Muruguppas, Falcks, Berkowitzs, and Hübschers accomplish the feat of being entrepreneurial generation after generation while simultaneously cultivating a functional family? How do these remarkable families overcome the sometimes valid danger noted by one of the greatest industrialists of the modern world, Andrew Carnegie,[8] who warned that "the parent who leaves his son enormous wealth generally deadens the talents and energies of the son, and tempts him to lead a less useful and less worthy life than he otherwise would."[9] After all, dimming the entrepreneurial spirit with easy access to wealth is only one of the golden handcuffs that enterprising families need to overcome.

It is not, however, necessary to wait generations to find enterprising families to learn from. For example, we also look at younger firms like Supreme Creations of the United Kingdom, in which regeneration of the enterprise took place when two generations joined forces. About two decades ago, Sri Ram established this company to make plain reusable bags out of jute, cotton, and canvas. With orders from UK supermarkets such as Asda, Tesco, and Sainsbury, as well as Nike and Top Shop of the United States, this was a successful start-up. However, growth accelerated when twenty-two-year-old Smruti Sriram, the Oxford-educated daughter of the founder, joined the business and introduced fashion designs. Within a short time, this family enterprise had over 50,000 clients around the world and was featured on the BBC news.[10]

What is necessary to innovate continuously and regenerate the enterprise to add value for customers? The hunger of working hard and smart must be developed, as at Supreme Creations, and then eventually sustained generation after generation. Investments must be made to avoid warfare among kin for dynastic legacy and power. Family turbulence through exits and entries caused by illness, death, divorce, marriages, adoptions, and similar events must be overcome. The inevitable disagreements about the direction of the business through the course of a family's history must be managed. Furthermore, the pace of growth of the enterprise and the family may not be in sync at all times. In some generations, the enterprise may grow much more rapidly than the family, while in others there may be no capable or interested family members to lead the firm. How are such mismatches and challenges handled to tame the dark side of working with loved ones while reaping the competitive advantages of a family team running a generational enterprise? In this book, we draw insights from

It is not, however, necessary to wait generations to find enterprising families to learn from.

companies like Caran d'Ache, Falck, Murugappa, Supreme Creations, and Tension to understand what exactly they do that enables their enterprises to flourish over generations of family leadership, while other companies succumb to the challenging consequences of change.

Technological and market changes are seen not just in bags, envelopes, pencils, steel, or banking but are evident in all industries. Yet against this backdrop of inevitable change, there are examples of enterprising families that seem to drink from the entrepreneurial fountain and have an unquenchable thirst to do things better in each generation, or at least to learn from and overcome mistakes in a generation.

Although they have often been major players in their chosen industries, such enterprising families are only now coming to public attention because of an increased awareness of the significant contributions of family enterprises to the economic and social well-being in most countries around the world. Depending on the definition used and the focal region, family businesses account for 60 to 98 percent of all economic activity.[11] Here are two standard definitions of family businesses, with slightly different emphases:

- Organizational entities in which either the individuals who established or acquired the firm *or* their descendants significantly influence the strategic decisions and life course of the firm, leading to success or failure of the business.[12]

- Businesses, whether public or private, in which a family controls the largest block of shares or votes and has one or more of its members in key management positions.[13]

Not only are these family firms major job creators, they have been found to be slow in downsizing when times are tough.[14] And employees notice. For example, today Dot Foods Inc. is the largest food redistributor in the United States, delivering more than 100,000 products to distributors across the country, employing over 4,000 workers, and having sales over $4.5 billion. But even when it was a small family business in the 1970s, founders Robert and Dorothy Tracy established an employee retirement plan[15] and maintained its no-employee-lay-off policy in the 1980s when they lost two major contracts. In 1999, the employees thanked the Tracy's by raising $25,000 to buy a fifty-three-foot trailer to not have to relocate outside of Mount Sterling, Illinois.

Some family enterprises crumble or explode. These examples are living proof that enterprising families can find ways to transmit the hunger for excellence and innovation across generations. In addition, they can find their own unique ways to socialize and develop the next generation of leaders to ensure that the family enterprise continues to succeed and grow beyond the founder's tenure. Nevertheless, sadly, it isn't hard to think of examples of businesses around the world that did not do so well. Books like *Family Wars*[16] capture the juicy estate battles of the Ford family, or the disagreements between the McCain or the

Enterprising families can find ways to transmit

the hunger for excellence and innovation

across generations.

Ambani siblings, or the struggles of the Spanish Álvarez family between father and sons,[17] or the Gucci family's saga of internal disputes. Yet such wrangling and squabbles are surely not the exclusive domain of legendary families that are in the public eye. Every community has its own set of unique family problems that lead to business exits.

It is not just the changes in the business environment or family disputes that can halt the generational continuity of a family enterprise. What is a family to do when the political environment is so unstable that they live under the constant threat of abduction and kidnapping? Or what if a change of regime brings with it mass deportations that force the family to leave in a hurry with few possessions and to start all over again in another part of the world? What happens if a natural disaster or war strikes, leaving the business in rubble and several key family members lost to eternity? What is to be done when there are no suitable heirs in the next generation or when there are so many members in the next generation that the business is not big enough to accommodate them all? And what is the best course of action when an enterprise was started not by one family but by two or more? Or when two or more equally capable siblings have very different visions of the future? In this book, we focus on families that have found their own unique and effective ways to deal with these kinds of scenarios while continuing to regenerate their enterprise over generations of leadership—enterprising families. Sometimes this regeneration happens only after the core enterprise dissolves and various family members start completely new businesses.

How Can This Book Help You?

What are we trying to do? In this book, we share insights drawn from published accounts of successful entrepreneurial leaders in family enterprises and our observations of and conversations with hundreds of business students and members of enterprising families. We aim to extract a handful of actionable ideas that are neither so abstract that they can be applied to anything with no visible consequence nor so particular that it would take a lifetime of searching to find the exact situation to which the advice is suitable.

How do we do it? We start by looking and reporting. Family firms are everywhere in the world, from small startups to companies with over one billion dollars in revenue, and they can be multigenerational organizations or may fail to even survive to, or through, the second generation.[18] Sometimes the death throes are precipitated by spectacular family blowups and at other times by inadequate leadership and adaption to changing conditions. One barrier to long-term survival is the failure of the current leadership to develop, instill, and select entrepreneurial leadership in the next (and succeeding) generations involved with the business. Whether members of the next generation take managerial or non-managerial ownership roles or not, if they don't have the urge and capacity to innovate as needed when the business and societal environment changes, their firms will not thrive.

Who is this book for? This book is for "enterprising families" everywhere. These are families in which each generation adds a layer of entrepreneurial contributions to the work of previous generations. We use the word *entrepreneurial* in the broadest sense, not just as starting new businesses. Instead, it may take the form of initiating value-creation activities, such as regenerating business processes, adding new products or services, opening new geographical regions, increasing distribution channels, improving financial methods, creating more effective marketing strategies or new channels or target segments, forming new partnerships, developing logical extensions of business lines (or disruptive ones), finding new sources of employees, and so on. To thrive over the years and changing circumstances, family enterprises, like all other organizations, need innovative entrepreneurial contributions. But not only must they be creative in the business sphere, they must also bring their entrepreneurial mind-set into their family system as well. Innovations in this sphere may take the form of finding creative ways to develop the entrepreneurial and leadership skills of all family members and to engage all family members in meaningful ways that align with their interests and strengths, as well as the needs of the enterprise. That might well include the conclusion that for some family members, full lives can best be lived outside the family enterprise.

> *One barrier to long-term survival is the failure of the current leadership to develop, instill, and select entrepreneurial leadership in the next (and succeeding) generations involved with the business.*

Where do we get our information? We use a variety of sources for examples. These include research journals, such as *Family Business Review* and the *Journal of Family Business Strategy* and practitioner-focused publications, such as *Family Business Magazine* and *Tharawat Magazine*. We also look at collaborative global research projects, such as the Successful Transgenerational Entrepreneurship Project (STEP) convened by Babson College, to understand the secrets of enterprising families around the world that master innovation in every generation; classic books that we reference throughout; and observations of family businesses, some by our colleagues along with our own. In addition, we bring in and apply relevant concepts and research findings from the business strategy, leadership, social psychology, team, and change literatures.

Who are we? Part of what makes this book different is what we share and the complementary skills we bring. We are both educators—teachers and researchers interested in entrepreneurial family firms. Allan grew up in a family business and completed his doctorate at Harvard Business School, studying Indian family firms in the 1960s. Pramodita (Dita) grew up in India surrounded by her enterprising family. Life's journey took her to Sierra Leone, Nigeria, the United Kingdom, Canada, and then to the United States. A graduate of the University of Calgary, her doctoral research focused on succession in Canadian family firms in the 1990s. With Frank Hoy she co-authored the text book *Entrepreneurial Family Firms*, which is used in courses around the world. Between us we have taught at undergraduate, graduate, and executive levels for over seventy years. Through this work experience, we have listened to the concerns, dilemmas, and excitement of our students from family business backgrounds. We have had many opportunities to speak with the incumbent leaders, often the parent or grandparent generations, and hear their perspectives, excitement, and anxieties about their family firms. As educators we address and meet family business leaders and advisors around the world. In our research on enterprising families we have had opportunities to interview, survey, and observe these firms up close, and we continue to learn from the work of others. Dita's consulting is atypical as it often takes the form of case studies she writes, student projects she guides, and the "go-to" person she becomes for many of her current and past students hailing from enterprising families. This happens with some of Allan's students also. Our middle-class family business backgrounds and deep familiarity with different cultures make it easy for our current and past students as well as their parents and grandparents to communicate with us. We are products of enterprising families that work hard to be entrepreneurial while achieving success on familial and business dimensions. What we have discovered speaks to families like ours, and we want to share our observations and insights with enterprising families who can benefit from these experiences and insights.

Although some of Allan's research, teaching, and consulting work has been with family businesses, most of it has focused on broader, more generic organizational issues: developing leaders, acquiring influence, building teams, and creating organizational change. He has worked in numerous countries with organizations in many different industries and of many different sizes, ranging from software startups to industrial conglomerates like General Electric. Several thousand managers have attended his executive education workshops and been a major source of his education. About 20 percent of his work life has been in leadership roles in academic institutions with low turnover, which have certain parallels to family businesses. Like family members, at times faculty members resist top-down direction. In such cases, the leader's ability to influence and inspire becomes even more important. Thus, together we bring deep knowledge about the intricacies of family business with broad knowledge of how to tackle the challenges of building organizations of all kinds, both from above and below.

What should you expect? When trying to understand how entrepreneurial skills and mind-set can be nurtured generation after generation, we find that size is not the most critical variable, as goals vary significantly. Some enterprising families focus their entrepreneurial energy on increasing the size and scope of their enterprise, while others prefer to stay small over generations. For example, by its fiftieth anniversary in 2012, Wal-Mart, founded by brothers Bud and Sam Walton as a single store in Rogers, Arkansas, had surpassed the 10,000 stores and 2 million employees mark. On the other hand, Johannes Klais Orgelbau GmbH & Co., the German organ building firm, has maintained its size at about sixty-five employees for over 100 years. Both are highly innovative companies that have successfully nurtured and grown entrepreneurs in every generation to remain world leaders in their respective industries. We learn from both, but our application focus is on the midsized family enterprises. Of course, no shoe fits two individuals perfectly—so we don't expect all of the insights we share to fit perfectly for you or your family. But we hope that some combination of ideas from different examples might be just what you need at this point in the evolution of your enterprising family.

It is clear to us that no one dominant factor creates entrepreneurs in every generation, but many small things coalesce to form a unique way that allows for each enterprising family to excel over generations. As you read, different things will strike you as suitable for your business and family, and for you personally, whether we pointed them out or you just observed them in a family or business we discuss. And you may well think of others in your world who would benefit from reading all or a portion of the book and discussing it with others in your generation. Continuous learning is good for keeping entrepreneurs developing in every generation—for those interested in leadership roles in the business or in the family.

In spite of mythology that lone entrepreneurial heroes create businesses by themselves, research[19] indicates that 80 percent of new ventures start as family firms with significant influence of family members on the human, social, and financial capital of the enterprise. And it

One of the few characteristics common to

almost all successful entrepreneurs is openness to

new ideas and experiences.

turns out that one of the few characteristics common to almost all successful entrepreneurs is openness to new ideas and experiences.[20] We hope this book provides a shortcut that helps a new generation to continue the entrepreneurial process for your family. Different parts of the book will spark ideas for you and them, depending on the life and career stage of each member, the nature of each member's experiences and aspirations, and the family's traditions and practices. And better yet, it might serve to launch discussions that prove fruitful for adapting its ideas to fit your situation.

How does it unfold? In this introduction we included a few examples of the companies that got us thinking about this topic and sources we found useful in developing our thinking. In the next six chapters we elaborate these observations at the individual (chapters 1 and 2), family (chapters 3 and 4), and organizational (chapters 5 and 6) levels. The odd-numbered chapters—1, 3, and 5—are the "what" chapters. In these, we build a short list of the practices—not always obvious—of successful entrepreneurial leaders, enterprising families, and entrepreneurial organizations respectively. The even-numbered chapters—2, 4, and 6—are the "how" chapters. These address the pathways to the best practices. In these chapters we share answers to your question: How precisely do enterprising families prepare individuals, families, and organizations for transgenerational success?

In presenting some of the patterns and pathways observed in enterprising families, we hope to enable you and your family to carve out a unique set of actions and strategies that are well suited to your individual and collective situations. Because families and businesses are living entities, existing in evolving and sometimes dramatically changing environments, with the passage of time the pathways that seemed perfectly suited for earlier stages of life of an individual, family, or business will likely need to be revised to protect, nurture, and grow the financial, intellectual, human, social and organizational assets. Each chapter provides a work sheet that prompts you and your family to reflect honestly on where you stand today in building entrepreneurs in every generation and to develop an action plan. Chapter 7 pulls together the book's main ideas and aims to help you choose a sequence that might fit the current conditions of your business; it also includes our "Iron Laws of Influence for Enterprising Families." We know there are ideas that can help you!

Chapter 1

Secrets of Successful Entrepreneurial Leaders

Long-term business survival depends on effective entrepreneurial leadership—not only from the founders, but equally importantly, from each subsequent generation that runs the enterprise. In this, the first of our "*what* it is and *why* it is important" chapters, we describe the essential characteristics of successful entrepreneurial leaders and the unique challenges and opportunities in building these attributes in family firms. Clarity on these points will help us to discuss in chapter 2 *how* next-generation members can take initiatives to grow their entrepreneurial leadership skills and *how* other members of their family can support such endeavors to nurture and grow entrepreneurs in every generation.

An Entrepreneurial Leader

At the core of entrepreneurial leadership is the constant willingness to seek unfilled needs and at least to consider whether it's possible to provide a usable solution. Identifying critical elements of such leaders is harder than it sounds. It is a lot like playing golf; from a distance it looks easy, but a new player's progress is thwarted by many hazards, only a few of which are actually visible. Just as golf is not a modified version of baseball, cricket, or soccer but a unique sport in itself, entrepreneurial leaders are also not simply entrepreneurs or leaders but a unique combination of both.

Such leaders can be introverted or extroverted, dominating or encouraging, determined or flexible. In fact some may not even be easily recognized as formal leaders even though they are highly influential. William McKnight is such an example.[1] Although his is not a household name, he is credited with laying the basic management principles for 3M. Founded in 1902 as a mining company, 3M had a rocky launch and became financially stable only in 1916. McKnight joined the company in 1907 as the assistant bookkeeper, over time rose to becoming its president, and retired in 1966 as its chairman. In 1948 he developed the following principles that helped propel this company into one of the most innovative companies in the world.

> **As our business grows, it becomes increasingly necessary to delegate responsibility and to encourage men and women to exercise their initiative. This requires considerable tolerance. Those men and women, to whom we delegate authority and responsibility, if they are good people, are going to want to do their jobs in their own way.**
>
> **Mistakes will be made. But if a person is essentially right, the mistakes he or she makes are not as serious in the long run as the mistakes management will make if it undertakes to tell those in authority exactly how they must do their jobs.**
>
> **Management that is destructively critical when mistakes are made kills initiative. And it's essential that we have many people with initiative if we are to continue to grow.**[2]

Notice the essential role of delegation, initiative, and mistakes in building an enterprise that is entrepreneurial at all levels over time. Nevertheless, media and historical accounts tend to depict entrepreneurs as confident solo swashbucklers who almost mystically came up with a brilliant insight, knew exactly how to proceed, and quickly developed a successful enterprise. In generational family firms, the failures, trials, and tribulations of the founding or earlier generations often acquire a heroic coating as the stories get transmitted over time. The path to success is seldom straight, with many experiments, failures, explorations, and small discoveries before success.[3] Usually success is achieved by incredible persistence, yet some very persistent entrepreneurs have doggedly marched over cliffs into the sea, ignoring the signals that they should have changed course.

Entrepreneurial leaders know that the success rate of new ventures is disappointingly low.[4] Yet research is unequivocal: first-generation family firms enjoy better financial performance than nonfamily firms, but from the second generation onwards the results are mixed.[5] That is, some do better while others flounder. Researchers continue to investigate why some family firms flourish over generations while others fold after the founders' tenure. Meanwhile, enterprising families that do well past the founding generation rely on building entrepreneurial and leadership skills of every generation.[6]

The path to success is seldom straight, with

many experiments, failures, explorations,

and small discoveries before success.

The good news is that entrepreneurial leadership skills can be developed with mindfulness and practice. Envisioning something new and delivering value—the crux of entrepreneurship—must be seamlessly integrated with inspiring others to suspend self-interest and reach high performance to make the leaders' vision a reality. Neither is sufficient without the other. An entrepreneurial leader needs to be equally comfortable leading and being led, staying on and changing course. Prudence lies in knowing when (and how) to lead and when (and how) to follow, when to start something new (and what this new thing should be) and when to stay on course. Often choices have to be made between two rights—such as achieving balance between the interests and dreams of the incumbent generation and those of the next generation, exploiting all possibilities of current markets while exploring future opportunities, fully engaging the most competent next-generation family *and* nonfamily members. Time and timing matter! *Ambidexterity*[7]—which literally means using both hands with equal ease—is the name of the game.

Not only must individuals at the helm of family enterprises simultaneously deploy entrepreneurial and leadership skills, but it is equally important that they prepare their organization[8] and family to be fertile grounds that encourage the development of these skills in the next generation. While we leave the discussion of family and organizational factors that enable such skill development to later chapters, let's turn our attention to what it takes to be an entrepreneurial leader.

Ambidexterity

Leadership effectiveness is about innovation and constant adaptation, but this is only part of the story. By definition, entrepreneurial leaders are innovative, finding new ways to fulfill unmet needs. This requires them to be flexible and intuitive. They must look closely at situations to decide whether a feasible solution exists or not. Although a combination of close observation of people and some analysis can make plain an unmet need, it often requires an intuitive leap to see the value-creating opportunity that is within the capacity of the entrepreneur and his or her resources. For family firms already in existence, exploration for new opportunities and exploitation of existing markets and products must be juggled simultaneously, requiring leaders to make judgment calls on how much time and resources to invest in each.[9] A flexible, intuitive approach must be complemented by equally strong disciplined analysis and precision. In generational family firms, the leaders must not only be clear about their own vision for the family enterprise but must also have the courage to acknowledge that the next generation's vision may not be fully synchronized with theirs. It is a delicate art to decide how far to pursue one's own vision and when to "let go" so as to make room for the next generation's vision to "take over." Wisdom lies in being sufficiently disciplined to achieve the precise combination of commitment and detachment that good judgment demands.[10]

An entrepreneurial leader needs to be
equally comfortable leading and being led,
staying on and changing course.

To better understand the ambidexterity of entrepreneurial leaders, let's look at two founders who grew their respective enterprises to global leadership positions before passing them to the next generation of family leaders. Both are remarkable in their own ways, influencing not just their industries but the lives of thousands of employees and customers. Notice their ambidexterity in switching between entrepreneurship and leadership and the ways their leadership styles may have changed as their enterprises grew from new ventures to global brands.

At age seventeen Fred Deluca launched what we now know as Subway Restaurants when his father's friend and a nuclear physicist—Dr. Peter (Pete) Buck—encouraged him to open a submarine sandwich store and lent him a thousand dollars to do so. Fred's motivation was to earn some money for medical school. In addition to Pete, Fred's parents, sister, and wife were all critical to the launch of this new venture in 1965 and its subsequent growth. Fred died shortly after celebrating the fiftieth anniversary of his company in 2015. By this milestone anniversary, he had led this family enterprise to become the largest submarine sandwich chain in the world with over 37,000 stores in over 100 countries. His sister Suzanne Greco, who has been involved in different roles with the company since its inception, is now the president and CEO of this family business.

While Subway's growth has been remarkable, it has not always been a smooth ride. Although apparently from the beginning Fred had the idea of offering healthier, less fattening food than existing fast-food chains and big dreams for expansion, the first two shops were not profitable. They were not in good locations, which were necessary for the success of sandwich shops. They required name changes, and the growth of the chain was much slower than the self-imposed goal of opening thirty-two stores in the first ten years. But Fred's dogged persistence and his partner's trust in him continued. Only when Subway finally moved to a franchise model did the company begin to expand more rapidly, achieving and often exceeding its goals.

Despite major law suits from franchisees, over the years Fred remained sufficiently hands-on to be sure that the company stayed in touch with the needs and interests of customers and that the shops maintained high quality, sanitary conditions, and excellent service.[11] With continuous incremental innovation, such as the addition of avocados on sandwiches, the introduction of Flatizza (a flat bread sandwich), and vegetarian Subway stores in India, this family enterprise has endured over time. An ambidextrous entrepreneurial leader, Fred could alternate between the dream and hands-on execution as needed.

Entrepreneurial leadership is not only the forte of founders in food services industry like DeLuca but also evident in other contexts. Like Subway, Lamborghini is today a world-famous brand. Might it surprise you to learn that it was only early in the 1960s that Ferruccio Lamborghini designed and manufactured his first car? While passionate about engines, he originally focused on repairing cars and motorcycles during World War II and then on designing powerful tractors to support the needs of local farmers in his native Emilia Romagna region. Only when Enzo Ferrari rebuffed him for proposing improvements to the Ferrari car did Lamborghini resolve to design and manufacture his own car. It took him nine months to design an elegant and powerful vehicle that was brought to market within two years. With a staunch belief in technical excellence and quality, Ferruccio led his enterprise through high and low times until he was in his seventies. Then one day, he is known to have unceremoniously handed over the keys and operations to his son Tonino, making himself available once a year for business-related discussions.

At the time of this unpretentious changing of the guard at Lamborghini, Tonino was a university student in his early twenties. Deeply familiar with the business because he had played in the premises as a child and worked there every opportunity he got, Tonino wanted to prove himself as an entrepreneurial leader who could build on his family's legacy. When the family sold its car brand to the Audi

Volkswagen group, he embarked into luxury watches. In an interview with *Tharawat*[12] he recalls that his father was not too keen on the idea of starting a fashion and luxury business. But, being a fair man with an acute sense of balancing between the needs and desires of the current and future generations, he said:

> **You know, I always did what I wanted to do, so why shouldn't you get your chance?**
>
> **(*Tharawat*, June 21, 2015)**

However, the senior Lamborghini emphatically reminded his son that the family name stood for technical know-how and mechanical excellence. Today, the third generation of the Lamborghini family is determined to continue to innovate and regenerate so they can keep ahead of the curve and contribute to their family enterprise.

Founders Fred DeLuca and Ferruccio Lamborghini were both able to evolve their entrepreneurial leadership styles as their companies grew. For the endurance and longevity of organizations under their charge, they knew to simultaneously focus on exploiting current markets while exploring new directions,[13] so as to build on the past while staying focused on the future. Without this combination, enterprises stagnate, flounder, fail to adapt to changing conditions, or slowly deteriorate beyond the tenure of such an individual. Only time will let us know if Fred DeLuca's Subway will fare well past his time at its helm after his recent death and if each subsequent generation of the Lamborghini family will continue to build on their founders' legacy.

The ambidextrous mind-set has been variedly referred to as "the genius of the 'And'" in *Built to Last* by Collins and Porras and "the opposable mind" by Roger Martin. Based on their decades of experience with multigenerational families around the world, Amy Schuman, Stacy Stutz, and John Ward look at *Family Business as Paradox*.[14] They conclude that the most enterprising families not only learn to manage such contradictions but find ways to turn them into secrets of success. For example, based on his forty-three years of experience leading the Murugappa Group of India, patriarch M. V. Subhiah notes that not only must they maintain a style befitting the size of their operations, but they must simultaneously preserve the moderation and humility that are core values for their family. While such integrative thinking is said to be at the core of great companies and visionary leaders, it is surely not easy to implement. Consider the comments of Rupert Murdoch, a second-generation member of a media family from Australia. A controversial yet highly successful entrepreneurial leader, he grew his father's news business into a global media conglomerate valued over $80 billion today. In an interview with *Fortune* he noted:

> **Print is going through a tough time. You've got to keep improving and competing in a new world, *as well as* keeping your old world going. ... I hope we are not wasting money, but we're spending it.**
>
> **(*Fortune*, April 28, 2014)**

Next-generation leaders like Rupert Murdoch, Suzanne Greco, and Tonino Lamborghini, who follow successful founders, face the dilemma of balancing tradition and innovation, creativity and operational excellence. It turns out that most people are (at best) naturally good at only one or the other. Some individuals, like Fred DeLuca, can learn to personally be good at both creating and building, while others have to recognize that when the opposite of their strength is called for, they have to find others—family members or outsiders—to complement them. In family enterprises that grow and sustain over generations, we can identify ambidexterity as five diametrically opposed core skills:

- Awareness of self *and* surroundings
- Building a dream *and* a team
- Influencing *and* directing
- Beginnings *and* endings
- Learning *and* unlearning

Let's look more closely at each of these core capacities.

Awareness of self and surroundings. Why do we first turn to self-awareness? People don't always think of this skill in relation to effective leaders. Yet there are at least three reasons to identify this capability when considering entrepreneurial leadership over generations. First, starting a new venture almost inevitably requires extraordinary time commitment and emotional investment from whoever initiates it. Even more energy and commitment are required when building something new and worthwhile within or related to an existing business, as the organizational culture and routines have already been established. Enterprising families understand that leaders from the next generation must operate in this context. When the activity demands total preoccupation, it is almost impossible to sustain it if it does not engage the personality, values, and passion—the core—of the leader. If individuals are forced into situations that do not tap what they care most about, they may find it hard to put in the necessary thought and effort or feel a vague malaise that they can't quite identify. But when there is alignment, it is possible to soar. Entrepreneurial leaders, therefore, have to be enough in touch with their inner being to choose to pursue only those opportunities that will completely capture them. This sense occasionally may be blindingly obvious, but more often it comes from diversity of experiences that lets someone identify what feels natural and effortless, a calling that fully engages an individual—that perfect "hand in glove" fit!

Second, the family history and legacy often weigh heavily on the psychology of the next generation of family members. For example, when he remembered the moment his father handed him the keys to the business, second-generation family member Tonino Lamborghini confessed to *Tharawat*: "Of course, I was scared. Here I was, still at university, and my father just hands me his life's work."[15] This feeling of responsibility and stewardship continues over generations, for the third-generation member of the Lamborghini family Ferruccio (named after the founder) remarked: "Yes, of course there is the need to live up to the expectations of this brand and this myth." Enterprising families know that if family members of the next generation start their career against such backdrop, they will need extra courage and opportunities to understand their true capabilities and interests. Casual interest in trying something out because there might be economic possibility often is not enough to overcome the aura of the family traditions. Genuine alignment with what really matters to next-generation leaders is the powerful energy source that can fuel these entrepreneurs when the going gets tough, which is inevitable when undertaking new initiatives.

Enterprising families and the individuals therein realize the critical importance of helping all family members to discover their true interests and talents. For example, Carole Hübscher, chair of Caran d'Ache's board of directors, whom you may recall from the last chapter, notes that "unless you are passionate, and you're really willing to join the family business, there is no point in forcing anyone to do so."[16] Research shows that four different reasons motivate next-generation members to pursue a career in their family firms. These are desire, obligation, greed, and need. While each decision combines these factors

Entrepreneurial leaders, therefore, have to be enough in touch with their inner being to choose to pursue only those opportunities that will completely capture them.

in different proportions, those propelled mostly by desire or obligation turn out to be much better leaders and performers, reporting higher levels of job satisfaction than those motivated by greed or need. Unfortunately, those who join their family businesses because of need (because they lack confidence in their ability to be productively employed in other spheres) are the weakest leaders of all.[17] In short, unless a person's heart is in it, it just won't work in the long term.

Third, successful leaders must know themselves in order to be able to engage needed others. It is impossible to do anything impactful alone, so leaders must be able to inspire, align, direct, motivate, and influence diverse and talented people. In order to do this effectively, it is critical for an individual to know his or her core strengths, limitations, interests, and even biases, as each succeeding generation must operate in an increasingly diverse work place. Think, for example, of what happens to a leader who at some stage of life has been deceived by trusting a friend too much. Seared into the leader's psyche is a deep distrust of people who appear to be friendly. While this suspicion can be helpful in sorting charlatans from others, it can also cause the leader to be so suspicious that good people are driven away or kept so at arm's length that they cannot give their best.

Most of us are susceptible to "The Danger of a Single Story," as eloquently described by notable Nigerian novelist Chimamanda Ngozi Adichie. She recalls[18] how characters in the stories she wrote as a child growing up in Nigeria mimicked those from the British and American books she read. Her characters were always white, had blue eyes, played in the snow, ate apples, drank ginger ale, and talked a lot about the weather, saying how lovely it was that the sun had come out. None of these made much sense in her Nigerian context, for she and most around her were black with brown eyes, ate mangoes, had never experienced snow, and had no reason to talk about weather, given that it varied little year round. Each generation has its own set of experiences, but the power of the stories about past experiences often have a deep impression on the next-generation members.

In a family business this might show up as an unwillingness to ever trust a nonfamily member or perhaps an unwillingness to trust any in-law who wants to be part of the family business. Conversely, another leader might have had bad experiences working for an autocratic boss and would come away from that experience determined to never give strong directions to anyone, assuming that everyone prefers the kind of autonomy that she or he longed for. Such a leader might write off as too dependent those subordinates who ask perfectly reasonable questions about direction or best methods, thus denying them a chance to learn and grow. Leading without self-awareness can thus get in the way of effectively making needed changes. As the McKinsey Consulting firm concluded from a recent study:

Many people aren't aware that the choices they make are extensions of the reality that operates in their hearts and minds. Indeed, you can live your whole life without understanding the

inner dynamics that drive what you do and say. Yet it's crucial that those who seek to lead powerfully and effectively look at their internal experiences, precisely because they direct how you take action, whether you know it or not. Taking account-ability as a leader today includes understanding your motiva-tions and other inner drives.[19]

Awareness of self also helps to build awareness of surroundings, both context and people, which in turn aids in selecting and inspiring a talented team. Many entrepreneurial leaders aren't particularly aware of their unique competencies and judge harshly those who cannot eas-ily do what they do naturally. Have you ever seen a numbers whiz glance over a column of figures and focus in immediately on the one that is incorrect or problematic? Because the person is so good at it, he or she is driven crazy if an otherwise competent subordinate either has

Genuine alignment with what really matters

to next-generation leaders is the powerful

energy source that can fuel these entrepreneurs

when the going gets tough.

no intuitive feel for such issues or takes four times as long to discover them. This situation can be made worse when the leader has deep ex-perience in the industry or business and is perpetually impatient with family members or employees who lack the same base of experience and therefore are not as efficient or proficient. Furthermore, if the pas-sionate, expert, and focused leader has earned self-confidence over the years and responds impatiently to those not as far along as they are or is sharply critical when pointing out what the others do not see, the next generation can end up not seeking or receiving positive feedback.

This makes it really hard for either generation to gain confidence and trust in the abilities of the other. The negative spiral continues, distancing the juniors from the family and firm.

Enterprising families that successfully prepare entrepreneurs in every generation realize the advantages of next-generation engagement and work hard at it. For example, Sylvia Shepard, a fifth-generation owner of Menasha Corporation and the chair of the Smith Family Council, notes:

> **Family business can have significant advantage over nonfamily business if they use their next generation as a barometer of change, and as a window into a new reality that the previous generation might not fully understand. If the family has done its job of preparing children for ownership and leadership, this next generation will act as the innovation engine for the company. They will provide the spark that enables the family firm to grow and prosper amid changing market realities. The family just needs to listen and be poised to respond to its young people.**[20]

Creating organizations where the leader, and everyone else, wakes up every morning excited and loving what they do is at the heart of what enterprising families aim for so that all family members experience a positive environment to identify a project or a venture to devote their energies toward. Such excitement is built into the core of such families regardless of whether they are start-ups or generational enterprises as indicated by these two examples. In 2011, sisters Zania and Rania Kana'an launched a website, Ananasa.com, to sell worldwide the unique products of the artists and craftspeople of the Middle East. When the company was in its infancy, both sisters worked in corporate jobs but were not satisfied, for they were not learning and could not realize their aspirations. They simply decided that they wanted to wake up every morning excited and loving what they did, thus they launched their own company.[21] Similarly, Charles S. Luck IV, the third-generation leader of the Luck Companies—one of the largest producers of crushed stone, sand, and gravel in the United States—wants "everyone to have a job at the company that exceeds their wildest dreams."[22]

When working in family firms, the family members of the next generation are under constant scrutiny not only from the senior generation but also nonfamily employees, customers, suppliers, bankers, and other key stakeholders. Going the extra mile while being in the public eye necessitates natural effort that comes only with strong awareness of self and others.

Building a dream and a team. At the core of entrepreneurial leadership is the ambidextrous capacity to envision a desirable future and paint a vivid picture of it that can inspire and excite others to build a team to help shape and then make the change. The imagined future can involve a new product, service, market, or process that is meaningful and valuable to at least some other people. Effective leaders can not only conceptualize and talk a good game but also have a knack to figure out how to actually bring the dream to fruition. Not only must they have a heightened sense of the steps necessary to make something real, they should also have a clear understanding of the required resources—those available and others where there are gaps. Finally, they must have the finesse to get past the obstacles: human, organizational, resource, legal, and others. The mere dreamers get written off as impractical big talkers, and those who only keep their noses to the grindstone without knowing why it is worth bothering and what they can create get written off as unimaginative plodders. While the dreamers see only the green blur of a forest without noticing the trees or leaves or rocks within, the doers without vision see only particular trees or leaves and not the pattern or potential of the whole.

Where does this dual capacity to both conceptualize and deliver come from? At times, it is a by-product of intimate familiarity with how people live or work, their problems and struggles, regardless of whether they themselves recognize it as a problem. For example, many are familiar with the grand vision of Steven Jobs at Apple, leading with a concept of aesthetically beautiful products that combine hardware and software that provide new access to music or the idea of mobile phones that do many functions not formerly expected in phones. An inspiring example from the other side of the globe is the story of Doctor Govindappa Venkataswamy, founder of the eye clinic

Aravind, which performs cataract surgery at no charge (patients pay what they like, up to market rate); the clinic has performed over 200,000 surgeries, saving thousands from eventual blindness. By 2010 the expanded Aravind system was seeing more than 2.5 million patients and performing more than 300,000 surgeries a year.[23] He was driven by a spiritual need to cure blindness and serve the poor, and his belief was so intense that over 20 family members, trained at the best Western medical schools, joined the company to do surgery at extremely low wages. But Aravind uses the most modern business practices to drive down costs, speed up all aspects of the surgeries, and raise quality, all of which make the model more viable. Higher throughput, for example, reduces the cost per operation, which allows profit even at low revenue rates and attracts more patients, even those who can go anywhere for their eye care. The combination of the dream and extraordinary team execution are amazing.

It is impossible to do anything impactful alone,

so leaders must be able to inspire, align,

direct, motivate, and influence diverse

and talented people.

Another kind of inspirational story involves co-founders L. S. "Sam" Shoen and his wife, Anna Mary Carty Shoen, who in 1945, with barely $5,000 in hand, set out to create U-Haul when the concept of renting a trailer from one city and returning it in another was unheard of.[24] The couple tried to move their own possessions from Los Angeles to Portland, Oregon, after Sam returned from the US Navy, but they could not find anyone who rented one-way trailers, thus spotting a market need and starting a new industry. According to their website, today "the annual mileage of North American U-Haul trucks, trailers and tow dollies would travel around the Earth 177 times per day, every day of the year." What a dream and remarkable growth in about seventy years! The Shoen family has had its share of trials and tribulations on the family dimension as Anna Mary died early after having six children, and Sam Shoen went through multiple marriages, having thirteen children who did not always get along. Today, two of Anna Mary's sons, Mark and Joe Shoen, are at the helm of this family enterprise.

The vision does not necessarily have to come from only one of the founders but can also be triggered by leaders of enterprising families from later generations, like that of Andrew Beale, managing director of Beales Hotel in Hatfield, England. This eighth-generation leader was the driving force behind the transformation of a lodge into the four-star Beales Hotel, catering to families desiring to gather together.[25]

> *Creating organizations where the leader,*
> *and everyone else, wakes up every morning*
> *excited and loving what they do, is at the heart of*
> *what enterprising families aim for.*

Family business can be a source of long-term dreams pursued over generations but also a series of filters that prevent the vision from taking root or keeping it totally out of reach. Let's talk about the generational pursuit of dreams first. Describing "shared dreams" of a family as the beacon that provides direction to the family enterprise over generations, a renowned family business educator, writer and advisor Ivan Lansberg notes:

The Shared Dream is a collective vision of the future that inspires family members to engage in the hard work of planning and to do whatever is necessary to maintain their collaboration and achieve their goals. It shapes the choices made at every point in the succession journey, from the company's strategic plan, to the selection of future leaders, to the type of the leadership structure it will adopt in the next generation.[26]

Enterprising families are often anchored by a shared dream of excellence in something—highest quality products, lowest prices, fastest delivery, or other areas. Efforts are made to imbue and modify the specifics of this broad anchoring dream so it becomes aligned with the core strengths and interests of each generation of leaders. For example, Gerry Ettinger founded Ettinger in 1934 to create luxury goods that would be known for quality and innovation not only in the United Kingdom but also in other European countries. When his oldest son Robert Ettinger came to the helm of the company, the shared family dream continued and expanded to markets beyond Europe. When Ettinger expanded into the Japanese market, some orders were rejected for not meeting customers' quality standards. As the company prided itself on quality products, Robert personally went to Japan to see what was wrong. He realized that each piece was inspected to ensure an identical number of stitches per inch. If they failed this demanding test, the pieces did not pass the inspection. Changes were made to the production process to meet these exacting standards. He says, "We know that when our Japanese clients approve, the rest of the world will be delighted."[27]

While in the Ettinger case, the family history worked to reinforce commitment toward the shared dream, in other instances the past can serve as a giant impediment. Families can become averse to risk in their desire not to jeopardize the family wealth, may avoid going into new directions even when the old industries are no longer vibrant, or choose not to trust nonfamily members in positions of responsibility even when no competent family is available to fill a role. A very strong founder can be so dominant that younger family members do not dare to think about doing anything different for fear that they

Going the extra mile while being in the public eye necessitates natural effort that comes only with strong awareness of self and others.

will not be given the chance to try, or even worse, be ridiculed for suggesting something that is different. The self-fulfilling prophecy of individual talent is confirmed by research in settings varying from elementary schools in San Francisco to trainees in the Israel Defense Forces, to employees in banking, retail sales, or manufacturing.[28] When a randomly selected set of students, trainees, or employees are labeled with positive descriptors such as "late bloomers" or "gifted" that indicate their superior abilities or talents, the behavior of these individuals and their superiors is unintentionally modified. The senior starts to pay more attention to the junior, raising expectations by showering praise and encouragement. The junior responds by taking more initiative and working harder, leading to superior performance that further reinforces the positive loop.

The reverse effect is equally strong. For example, for many years women and minorities in organizations appeared to have low aspirations. This attitude was reasonable if people lived in an era when they were highly unlikely to be given responsibility or advancement no matter how talented they were. But their aspirations rose dramatically when some chance or circumstance gave (or thrust upon them) more responsibility.[29] Sadly, powerful incumbent leaders often perceive this kind of reaction to low opportunity by juniors as evidence that no one in the family is ready to take over, which perpetuates their discouraging behavior. Such attitudes might well be a result of some particular family or family business event where things went wrong, with extreme caution overlearned as a result. Of course at times such caution can serve as the brakes that help preserve a family company through tough economic crises. But enterprising families make mindful efforts to trigger the imagination and aspirations of each generation.

But even vivid dreams require others to make them real. A central yet sometimes overlooked skill is the art of deciding who else is needed, recruiting them by helping them connect to the dream, then working with them to at least launch the first phase of implementing the dream. It is no small feat to find a way to talk so vividly and compellingly about something new that others who are needed for their knowledge, talent, resources and connections—family members or not—want to join. But someone without the capacity to attract and work with people who have complementary skills will find it hard to build an organization.

Sometimes the only other key player is a spouse or sibling, sometimes a son or daughter or parent, and at other times a close friend or friends; related or not, the key players must have sufficient trust to move forward. Family members can have an advantage because of their shared experience and trust when it exists. For example, beyond their academic training and work experience, part of what has allowed the Kana'an sisters to successfully build not only their first venture Ananasa.com, but also their second one, ChariCycles.com,[30] is the trust between them. As Rania explains:

"Zaina brings a lot to the creative side. She has that Salvador Dali type imagination and implements it in the business. This is great because she is mainly in charge of marketing." Zaina in turn ... muses, "I can't visualize not having Rania in my team; to me she symbolizes total honesty. Because we are sisters we can be totally honest with each other and there is much less miscommunication." Both ... agree that it is mainly the high degree of respect that they have for each which makes the collaboration successful; that and ... aware[ness] of each other's skills and shortcomings ... Rania ... explains that the advantage of their collaboration stems chiefly from their differences and from how their characters complement each other ... "The good thing about our relationship is that we forgive each other really quickly. We have our conflicts out when they happen and then know to let them go quickly. I think this is something I would recommend for anyone working with family members."[31]

In other instances, accomplishing dreams requires building a team of talented outsiders. Working *in* a team and working *through* others are quite different skills. To be effective team members and leaders requires an individual to be adept at influencing as well as directing and knowing the time and place for each. We turn to this ambidexterity next.

Influencing and directing. Incumbent leaders have considerable power to invent and assign roles, determine and administer pay, reward the desired or punish the undesired behavior, and promote or terminate employees. With authority, however, comes responsibility. These leaders must also make difficult decisions and forge ahead under great uncertainty, knowing well the painful consequences if they miscalculate. These leaders control the budget and strategic direction of the company, often serve as the emotional anchors and crucibles of values that help distinguish right from wrong, and are the central nodes of important social networks. Thus, they have the ability to provide or withhold financial, social, and even emotional support. In families, there is ample research to indicate the root cause of sibling rivalry is the desire for the precious yet limited resource of parental attention.[32]

Enterprising families understand the difference between directing and influencing. Each has an important role to play in the operations of a business. Directing is geared toward making sure the current projects are completed and products delivered in time to existing customers. Influencing, on the other hand, engages the whole person to give his or her very best effort and take the initiative to ceaselessly fine tune so things are done a bit better every day. Getting such attention from the very core of another individual builds on empathy and a good understanding of the aspirations and dreams of the other. There is a difference between the *specifiable* part of the job, which is captured in job descriptions, and the *unspecified*, fuzzier component of the job that is left to discretion. Rarely does excellence and true difference come from handling the specified components exceptionally well. Instead, it is what is left to our discretion that helps build entrepreneurs in every generation.[33] Both directing and influencing require finesse in communications. Such articulation requires practice. Perhaps even 10,000 hours of practice is required to build outstanding skills, as Malcolm Gladwell argues in *Outliers*.

Increasingly leaders need to gain cooperation when giving directions not sanctioned by their formal role, or they will be readily ignored. In any organization, even the powerful top person will have to deal with key outsiders who are not obligated to listen. Examples may include government officials who can create or implement regulations, bankers or other funders, boards of directors, vendors, and certainly customers—all of whom are under no obligation to accommodate the interests and desires of the organization's leader. In complex organizational settings, with multiple technologies and specialties, various product lines, diverse locations, and so on, leaders increasingly must rely on their ability to influence the people who may work for the same overall company but have differing expertise, objectives, ways they are measured, allegiances, ways of working, or basic views of what behavior will best help the organization.

While the dreamers see only the green blur

of a forest without noticing the trees or leaves

or rocks within, the doers without vision see

only particular trees or leaves and not

the pattern or potential of the whole.

The capacity to influence is a central requirement for entrepreneurial leaders to get things done in any organization,[34] but it takes an even more profound meaning in family firms. By the time members of the next generation begin their career in family firms, the rules and operational practices are already in place. Family members who may or may not have a significant involvement in the business may feel entitled to voice strong opinions simply by virtue of their hierarchical position in the family structure. And when they do have ownership roles, even without executive responsibilities, their sense of entitlement often becomes even stronger and more legitimate. For example, the Illinois Consolidated Telephone Company was founded as a small-town telephone company in 1924. Richard A. Lumpkin, the fourth generation to lead this family enterprise, faced significantly different dynamics than his father did when he took over as the sole owner of the company. Upon the death of Richard's father, the stock was passed to fifteen family members who were scattered across the country.

Enterprising families are often anchored by a shared dream of excellence in something.

While Richard was named the trustee of his father's trusts and had effective control of the company and the board voted him to succeed his father as the CEO, suddenly he found himself in a position of having to convince many more family members before he could take any significant initiatives in the company.[35] Given the overlapping roles between business and family, this had to done rather delicately to avoid awkwardness in family gatherings or (worse still) to end up with distressed family members whom he might have to buy out. Thus, as the next-generation leader he had to learn to hold discussions with and often times influence the key stakeholders in powerful positions.

Not only is the number of stakeholders often much larger in family enterprises, the opportunities to build directing and influencing skills can be a major challenge. Too often the leadership roles in both the family and the business are held by the same people or members of the same generation.

The members of the next generation may find themselves in *vice* president positions rather quickly, often cutting short the necessary learning time of each previous stage of their career ladder. However, they then often spend much longer time in this penultimate position than their counterparts in nonfamily firms.[36] This is largely due to the *multigenerational stack-up* caused when the incumbent generation lives longer and healthier lives and has extended leadership tenures.[37] While the incumbent leaders are well positioned to build their directing and influencing skills, how do enterprising families create opportunities for the next generation to hone these skills? In the next chapter, we will discuss some ideas that such families have found helpful.

Beginnings and endings. The popular image of entrepreneurs is that they create something new and are huge risk takers. As we discuss below, both these images have a bit of a counter side to them. While entrepreneurs often do create something new, as Joseph Schumpeter argued, within each creation lies some *destruction* or the ending of something—be it resources in the form they earlier were, time of the individuals involved, or the market before the new creation. Although Schumpeter focused on the economic structure, the concept applies equally well to new beginnings in family firms, as these new beginnings often come at the cost of some exits that help to free up time and resources to invest in the new.

Taking entrepreneurial action is conditioned as much by attitude towards risk as it is by objective risk. Entrepreneurial leadership is unlikely to occur or to be passed along to younger generations without some kind of belief that preserving the status quo is not necessarily safe and that finding a new and better way to do something is not automatically prohibitively risky. Past decisions, even when successful, are seldom good forever. Successful entrepreneurs, in order not to squander scarce assets, often must be willing to end an activity— a project, a business line, a product, a once promising expansion, a job, a location—no matter how fond of it they are. "That's my baby" can be a beautiful sign of deep investment and loyalty or a of tragic unwillingness to let go. As Danny Miller's book *The Icarus Paradox* notes, the very same things that created success, when taken to excess, can cause decline and failure.

Over generations, some family firms stay in the same industry in which they were founded, while others evolve into different industries, markets, products, or size. Regardless of how much the enterprise changes over its life course, the path of generational family firms is marked by endings or exits to make way for the new as the context and conditions change. Paradoxically, even standing still in the same location and industry requires change. For example, while Bremen Casting, a machine shop started by three foundry men in a garage in 1939 to make castings for furnace grates, has stayed in the same location and business for over seventy-five years, the company looks very different today. Although still based in its original building, the facility has expanded from 5,000 to 130,000 square feet. It has developed from three men working in a garage in the 1930s, to a factory run on manual labor in the 1960s, to an automated foundry that runs 24 hours a day in 2014. James Brown, the fourth-generation president of the company, remarks that

It is what is left to our discretion that helps build entrepreneurs in every generation.

although Bremen Castings is in the same business in which it started, "the company itself looks very different. Reinvention of the company has been key to its survival."[38] In this company, each generation reenergized the business. With each evolution, the previous era ended. Thus leaders must have not only the wisdom to make changes and investments but also the ability to handle the closures as well as transitions. Such changes test the mettle of two generations, requiring the baton to be passed not only in terms of leadership change but also what each leader brings to the company. Practice is needed for both—to start something new and to end the ways of the past.

In the next chapter, we share how some enterprising families are creating opportunities for members of the next generation to experience and learn the skills of new beginnings and endings while weighing the risks and returns.

Learning and unlearning. Often leaders are expected to know everything already. This may well be close to the truth in simpler businesses like small family farms, in which methods were passed down over generations and experienced leaders did know a lot more than most other people. And those who have found an industry they love that deeply taps their inner spirit can acquire deep expertise that makes it easy for them to forget they are ever learning something new even while using their wisdom. But in the contemporary world, almost everywhere, things are changing too rapidly for any one person to have all of the necessary knowledge—and indeed, often no one possesses the knowledge because no one yet knows a solution to the problem being addressed. Whether it is parents who must rely on their children to help them learn how to use new technologies such as the personal computer, portable devices, and instant messaging or other social media, or business people who have to bring in educated specialists to determine customer desires, select appropriate equipment, design new processes, or even figure out how to hire qualified, educated specialists, expertise is much more widely distributed than it once was.

Nevertheless, there are often gaps between the perception of leaders and those who are supposed to follow them as to just how much the formal leader is expected to know. Some leaders can try to preserve the image of being all-knowing, invulnerable, settled, superior, or arrived, and this attitude is often fed by followers who perpetuate the expectations. Past success can often cause leaders to overestimate their ability to get it right, making it hard for them to acknowledge that *"what got them here won't get them there."*[39] Unlearning the ways of the past, even though they brought success, is perhaps even harder than learning anew, as illustrated by the reactions of two generations of Lumpkins from the Illinois Consolidated Telephone Company mentioned earlier. When Richard Lumpkin went to his father to suggest that they create a holding company so they could branch into the unregulated business, the eighty-five-year old father remarked: "Son, I wouldn't be for that even if I thought it was a good idea." While the senior Lumpkin had taken many risks during his sixty-year tenure in the leadership position, at that stage of life he was not prepared to take more overt risks or learn anew. And when most of the spinoffs started by her son in the first five years of his leadership lost money, Richard's mother said, "I don't understand why we didn't just stick with the telephone business," to which he responded, "I didn't think we ever left. This is the telephone business. It's just changed." To stay a step ahead of the wave, he, his family, and his employees had to be prepared to "unlearn everything we've (they) learned in the past 100 years."[40] But such learning and unlearning is a difficult course to master.

We have seen leaders of gigantic corporations and of corner grocery stores caught in the operational everyday trap, leaving little time to think of new undertakings. Yet we are encouraged to see enterprising families like the Scherrers of Switzerland[41] that established a plumbing and roofing workshop in 1896 that has grown into a highly successful brand found on most well-known buildings of Zurich. Beat Scherrer, a fourth-generation descendant of the founder, explains that a great part of their family's success has relied on ensuring the enterprise was always in young hands. For example, he had only worked in his family's business for five years when his father and uncle handed over the leadership of the enterprise to him. The next generation always gets a shot early on in their business, and thus no one holds on to the top position until death. In fact, although no member of the fifth generation is interested in running the enterprise's operations, Beat plans to turn over the leadership to nonfamily members next year when he turns sixty and the company celebrates its 120th anniversary.

In conclusion, regardless of which of the ambidexterity skills we consider—awareness of self and surroundings, building a dream and a team, influencing and directing, or new beginnings and endings—continuous learning is necessary. Although it is possible to identify many more competencies that would help entrepreneurial leaders in family businesses, with these they can keep learning and adapting to whatever comes along. In the next chapter we will look at some of the tactics that enterprising families are using to enhance the entrepreneurial leadership skills of each member of their family.

WORK SHEET 1

Entrepreneurial leaders are on a continuous learning cycle working each day to develop ambidextrous skills discussed in this chapter. Use this work sheet to:

1. Rate yourself on the skills listed in the first column in the following table, using a 1 to 5 scale.

2a. Ask a trusted member of the other generation to rate your skills. If you are a member of the junior generation, ask a senior generation member to rate your skill level. If you are a senior generation member, ask a junior to rate your skill level.

2b. Ask a trusted nonfamily member who knows you well to rate your skills.

3. Compare the results in perceptions in Steps 1, 2a, and 2b. Indicate similarities (S) and discrepancies (D) in scores. Discuss the reasons behind these, identifying your strengths and skills that need development.

4. Highlight each skill that is important to you and that needs development. Set a measurable goal for yourself.

5. List each skill that needs development. Commit in writing to what you will accomplish, by when, and how.

Using the scale below, rate yourself on each question. 1 = Poor 2 = Fair 3 = Good 4 = Very Good 5 = Excellent	STEP 1 Self-perception	STEP 2a* Rating from trusted other generation member	STEP 2b* Rating from a trusted nonfamily member	STEP 3 Indicate similarities (S) and discrepancies (D) in scores	STEP 4 Desired goal level of important skills
Level of clarity about your* innate strengths					
Level of clarity about your career interests					
Level of awareness of objects around you					
Level of awareness of people around you					
Level of clarity on what you want to accomplish in your career within the next five years					
Level of clarity with which you think of new projects or ideas					

Using the scale below, rate yourself on each question. 1 = Poor 2 = Fair 3 = Good 4 = Very Good 5 = Excellent	STEP 1 Self-perception	STEP 2a* Rating from trusted other generation member	STEP 2b* Rating from a trusted nonfamily member	STEP 3 Indicate similarities (S) and discrepancies (D) in scores	STEP 4 Desired goal level of important skills
Level of clarity in figuring out smaller pragmatic steps to accomplish your projects					
Level of clarity with which you can explain your new project ideas to others					
Level of clarity with which you can explain the steps to accomplish a project to others					
How good are you at engaging others to work with you?					
How good are you at influencing your peers?					
How good are you at influencing your seniors?					

Using the scale below, rate yourself on each question. 1 = Poor 2 = Fair 3 = Good 4 = Very Good 5 = Excellent	STEP 1 Self-perception	STEP 2a* Rating from trusted other generation member	STEP 2b* Rating from a trusted nonfamily member	STEP 3 Indicate similarities (S) and discrepancies (D) in scores	STEP 4 Desired goal level of important skills
How well can you direct juniors?					
How well do you listen to others?					
How good are you at learning new things on your own?					
How good are you at learning from others?					
How good are you at starting new projects or ventures?					
How good are you at ending projects or ventures?					
How good are you at adapting to new circumstances?					

*For rating by other family members or nonfamily members, please change you/your to your name.

STEP 5: Make a list of the skills that you would like to develop, by when, and how.		
Skills	Development Plan	Time Line

Chapter 2

DEVELOPING ENTREPRENEURIAL LEADERSHIP SKILLS

T homas Alva Edison held 1,093 patents over his life time, having at least one new patent every year for sixty-five consecutive years. Best known for inventing the phonograph and motion picture camera and successfully commercializing electric lighting, he symbolizes the relentless pursuit of innovation and continuous improvement. "I can never pick up a thing without wishing to improve it," he once remarked.[1] While Edison is unique in his accomplishments, enterprising families try to imbue his mind-set of ceaseless fine-tuning and ability to inspire others in every family member. Each generation views itself as the family steward responsible for building on the legacy of its predecessors. Continuous adaptation and improvement is the core of the stewardship mind-set.[2] Some long-lasting progressive families do indeed accomplish this state where entrepreneurial instincts become a norm.[3] However, this state is not a destination but a journey of continuous learning in which both senior and junior generations play an integral part. Focusing on the development of intellectual, emotional, and social skills of members of the next generation, enterprising families embrace whole-person learning.[4] Opportunities for such learning present themselves in five forms.[5] The end of this chapter contains a work sheet that lets you keep tabs on what you already do well in terms of each learning form and where it might be helpful for you to build some more skills.

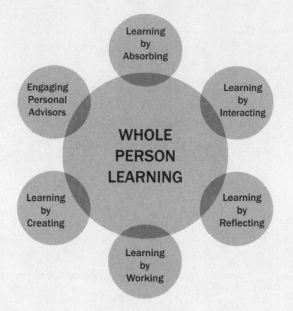

Figure 2.1. Six Forms of Learning to Develop Entrepreneurial Leadership Skills

Learning by Absorbing

An advantage of a family that runs a business is that family members can absorb a lot of information just by being alert, by listening and observing. Often by listening to family conversations younger members can understand instincts about self and surroundings; learn how to evaluate, take, avoid, and deal with risks; see the values that guide decision making; and learn the words, tone, and gestures that encourage others to follow a leader. Some younger people are naturally drawn toward the discussion of such issues, while others are not terribly interested and easily drift away into their own thoughts. Of course, familial norms vary in terms of discussing business or family matters around children. Regardless of these norms, in today's fast-paced lives, it takes discipline to be available for family gatherings and to be "in the moment" during them to reap the unique learning benefits from family members' experiences.

The power of gathering over a meal transcends the history and geography of humanity, as sharing food has a profound effect on building relationships and understanding the others' perspectives. How often meals are shared together varies over the life cycles of families and individuals. Robert Tracy, a father of eight, was thirty-four in 1960 when he started a modest powdered-milk delivery service in Mount Sterling in western Illinois. Today, Tracy's Dot Foods Inc. is the largest food redistributor in the United States, delivering more than 100,000 products to distributors across the country, employing over 4,000 workers, and having sales exceeding $4.5 billion. Joe Tracy, son of Robert and Dorothy and the current president and chief operating officer of Dot Foods, recalls observing that his father loved to talk with employees and customers. And every other month, his mother would invite a different group of customers to the company to listen to what they were doing right and how they could improve their services. In an interview with the *Family Business Magazine,* he explains how dinner conversations in their family reinforced the notion that while family harmony was Rule #1, family members could disagree and debate with candor without being destructive:

We love to debate and don't shy away from conflicts. ... Our parents often didn't see eye-to-eye. We learned from listening to them argue at the dinner table that people could have different perspectives and still share a common vision. Our comfort level with disagreements was a good preparation for the business.[6]

It is not necessary for such quality family time to be spent around meals, however. Each family is unique and can arrange some form of regular get-togethers that facilitate the flow of conversations. Families can share and listen to stories and dreams during walks or drives, vacations or celebrations, or even sad family gatherings. The rhythms of some families naturally carve out times for easy flowing conversations. In such cases, all that is needed is to be an active participant and think of ways to deepen the experience and mutual learning. If the current rhythms of a family do not encourage such conversations, there is a unique opportunity to organize new activities that bring the family in close range to listen to and observe each other. Entrepreneurial leaders enjoy starting something new and inspiring others to energetically follow along. Wherever a gap exists, an opportunity awaits.

Junior generation family members often have more influence on the family's choices than they may realize. If you want to start something new to enhance the active sharing and listening in your family, you have in your favor the human tendency that the American social psychologist James Pennebacker labeled the "joy of talking."[7] In an experiment, he divided strangers into small groups. Each group was given fifteen minutes to talk about their members' favorite subjects— school, career, hometown, and other topics. After the assigned time, the participants individually reported how much they liked the group and how much they learned about other group members. Interestingly, those who talked more reported liking their group more. The talkers also felt they learned more about the group, even in cases when most members in their group did not say much.

"Storytelling is a very old human skill that gives us an evolutionary advantage," notes the celebrated author Margaret Atwood. For example, "[I]f you can tell young people how you kill an emu, acted out in song or dance, or that Uncle George was eaten by a croc over there, don't go there to swim, then those young people don't have to find out by trial and error."[8] Families have stories about their history and its players, its conquests and its defeats. These narratives shed light on the business and its cast of characters, values held sacrosanct by the family, lessons learned, and pitfalls to avoid. In a study of forty-one wineries in Sardinia, researcher Nadine Kammerlander and her colleagues[9] discovered that a "founder" focus in family stories deters innovation by later generations as it encourages sticking with the ways of the past. In contrast, when "family" is the focus of the stories, innovation by next-generation members is enhanced as the past success inspires them to make future-focused decisions.

Stories of some enterprising families, like the SC Johnsons, are shared through films providing a glimpse into how each generation liberates the next to make future-focused decisions. In the film *Carnaúba: A Son's Memoir*, fourth-generation leader Samuel C. Johnson (Sam) received a posthumous letter from his father, who died in 1978, encouraging him to run the company as he felt was right for his people and to pay no heed to those who complained that he was not running it as his father had done. This led Sam to conclude that "as a son I shouldn't worry too much about whether I have lived up to the expectations of my father ... but whether we as fathers live up to the expectations of our children,"[10] thereby reinforcing the stewardship mind-set in this remarkable family.

In enterprising families, some stories lurk on the surface and appear with ease during family gatherings ... but more digging is needed to surface other, perhaps more interesting stories.

A lot can be learned simply by spending time and listening to family stories. Research suggests that an attentive listening skill makes us more attuned to others' thoughts and feelings as we become adept at picking cues from words and body language used,[11] even noticing the changes in facial expressions during a conversation. It is amazing how much we can learn in a short time if we just let people speak, then listen with our head for the evidence *and* with our heart for the emotions.[12] Mindful listening is a skill that needs to be cultivated, however, as the human tendency to talk resides within each of us. And it is hard to really listen when talking or planning the next thing to say, or reaching out to check the electronic message that just arrived. You might want to try the little exercise of sitting quietly and mindfully at home or in school or a workplace and simply absorbing what is going on around you. Try for five minutes, then increase to ten, and then to twenty, and see how the voice of silence becomes louder and you start to see and hear things you never knew existed around you. Don't forget to keep tabs on when you switch from an alert, conscious mode to a more introspective, meditative mode. Slowly, such practice helps to build awareness of self and the surroundings—the ambidextrous skills useful for entrepreneurial leaders. While such awareness is surely the primary benefit of absorbing by attentive listening and observing, there are secondary benefits to all other ambidexterity dimensions discussed in the last chapter. Examples include contemplating and clarifying one's dreams and better understanding current or potential team members, learning the influence tactics in use, and different ways to handle new beginnings and endings, entries and exits.

Learning by Interacting

In enterprising families, some stories lurk on the surface and appear with ease during family gatherings. Attentive listening is sufficient to absorb the nuances of such conversations. But more digging is needed to surface other, perhaps more interesting stories. One possibility is to ask questions. "But not all questions are equivalent," notes Edgar Schein in his book *Helping*. He contends that the social art of asking questions—what we ask whom, how we ask, where we ask, and when we ask—is essential to build trusting relationships and ensure better communications and collaborations.

Schein has proposed[13] that to draw someone out and to get an honest response, it is necessary to engage in "humble inquiry," that is, to ask questions based on curiosity and interest in the other person—in other words, questions for which we don't already know the answers. He argues that for a question to lead to an honest response, two conditions must be met. First, an individual must believe that the person asking the question is genuinely curious and interested, and second, he or she must have an open mind to receive the information shared. Apparently most of us tend to be quite adept at spotting an insincere question, regardless of how it is phrased, and knowing when the recipient is not ready to receive information. The diagnostic we often use to decide whether or not there is a genuine interest is how well he or she hears the response and the follow-up questions asked. Family members, in particular, deeply understand each other, know when a question is asked sincerely or not, and sense when a family member has stopped listening.

Is there a set of standard questions that are more likely to solicit honest responses from family members or from those working in and with your family business? The short answer is no. But some questions are better than others. The aim is to ask questions that do not influence the content or form of the responses. Exploratory, open-ended questions that encourage the other person to tell his or her story in an unbiased way are better than those that can be answered with a simple yes or no. Questions that draw on the experience of other family members work best because they imply that their experience is important and valued. Such questions—usually short in nature—avoid inadvertently steering the conversation in a particular direction and instead leave it open for the respondent to relax and share information with ease.

Venerated talk show host Charlie Rose, who has spent almost four decades interviewing heads of states, industry leaders, and movie stars, was asked how he developed his light touch that allows his subjects to lead a conversation. He noted:

> **It's mostly about listening. It's surprising to me how many people in this business don't listen. They'll ask something that the person has already spoken to because they're thinking about their list of questions. I'm never that: I'm always in the moment. I do a lot of research but the conversations are spontaneous.**

And, on his famous pregnant pauses in interviews, he says:

> **You have to let a conversation breathe, let it have space. … I think I help people explain themselves by the nature of the engagement, asking the right questions, making it feel like there's no one there but the two of you, being silent for a moment, and then saying, "But is that all?"**[14]

Here are some triggers to open up or build family conversations related to business.

- "Tell me about …"
- "Really, tell me more …"
- "Go on …"

- "Like what? Can you give me an example?"

- "How did our family get into …"

- "How did we change directions …"

- "What might be some interesting future directions for us?"

- "What did we (our family) do about that?"

- "What did she (or he) do then?"

- "How did you (or our family) feel about that?"

- "How would they have reacted if we had told them how we felt?"[15]

Such questions are useful to learn the basics about a family and its business, although if you ask and don't really listen to the answers, it makes things worse. Faking interest kills relationships and closes off others. But once these basics are learned, the questions that start with *why* enable deeper levels of understanding. *What, when, where, how,* and *who* questions shed light on a focal event, the time it happened, its location and the process through which it happened, and who the players were.[16] But only *why* questions explain the subject and lead us to a deeper understanding of it and the underlying social, psychological, physical reasons for events and decisions.

Try this. Ask a family or nonfamily member involved in your family business a question starting with *what, when, where, how,* or *who*. Listen carefully to the answer. And then ask a follow-up question starting with *why*? Notice what you learn from the two responses. Remember the purpose of asking these questions is to interact with the person, not to immediately refute the answers.

Members of enterprising families learn a lot about each other's core and evolving interests and needs through regular interactions. They are therefore better positioned to identify mutually beneficial opportunities for next-generation members to engage in the family enterprise. For example, Brian Butler,[17] a third-generation member of Dublin Cleaners of Ohio, a company with a good reputation for cleaning bridal wear, was leading an independent software company when his father Greg asked for his help on a one-year project to improve the systems of their dry cleaning company. Brian had spent a lot of time with his father when Dublin Cleaners was under construction, so he was attracted to this project to help his parents' company. By collaborating with another software company, he created an identifying bar code that could be attached to the clothes, thereby improving accuracy without increasing the labor. Next, he added a robotic order assembly system that allowed customers to track their orders through the company website or a smart phone app. While working on these projects, Brian got so involved in the family firm that he joined it full time. Under his leadership, Dublin Cleaners expanded from one to five locations. His mother commented that "Brian really took the business into the twenty-first century. Everything he has done has really made it (Dublin Cleaners) leaps and bounds ahead of other dry cleaners."

Faking interest kills relationships and closes off others.

Families vary in their prevailing beliefs and norms regarding hierarchy and equality across generations. In some families the norm is for the senior generation or elders within the same generation to have the last word, and top-down direction flows easily. In such contexts, how can junior family members establish their voices without sounding disrespectful, particularly when opinions differ? Examples of differing views might include career-related decisions such as studying a field that is different from familial norms or expectations; working in another company, industry, or country after graduation; starting in a particular position in the family business; asking for formal evaluations or promotions; or launching a new venture at the start of a career.

It is helpful when family members have sensitivity and understand that perspectives often vary because of differences in life stages and experiences. When building a case for one's position, it helps to frame the discussion around *why* unorthodox steps are needed or *how* the proposed changes are likely to benefit the enterprising family. Every course of action will have not only some pros and cons but also contingencies, that is, reasons things could go wrong. Inevitably, it helps to think from the other's perspective and to understand why they may have reservations and what those might be. If someone is prepared to present logical, fact-based responses to such reservations when they come up, not only does that person increase the likelihood of getting a favorable response but such thoughtfulness helps to earn the respect of influential people. It is not only the content of what to present and the preparation that goes into it but also how it is presented. Some school-going members of the next generation find it helps to

The questions that start with why
enable deeper levels of understanding.

join debating clubs or case competitions, as that enables them not only to build their analytical skills but also to become more comfortable in thinking on their feet and articulating their position clearly. And senior family members might get better responses if they are willing to explain the reasons for their views and (when possible) the history that has led them to their firm views.

Through thoughtful listening, observing, and asking, family members can understand why employees follow family or nonfamily members in leadership positions and why some individuals are better at coming up with new ideas while others are better at executing them. Over time, such distinctions help them to become adept at both creating new possibilities and leading people. Both take practice. Seniors in enterprising families support the building of these skills and the development of all voices even if they hold different views.

Learning by Reflecting

Learning to absorb and interact with the world around is a good starting point for next-generation members, as there is a lot to learn from the surroundings. However, amidst the din of past success and the prevailing familial norms of hierarchy, it is perhaps more challenging to discover one's true passion(s) and learn to think independently. Yet, such discovery lies at the heart of developing entrepreneurial leadership skills, given the uniqueness of each individual's talents and interests, upon which excellence must be built. Entrepreneurial excellence demands a 24/7 attention span, which is difficult to sustain without an alignment of interests and talents.

Research on failed successions in family businesses[18] indicates that mindlessly following the past is as harmful as the rebellious rejection of it. Families that succeed across generations align the interests and ambitions of the next generation with the business, and vice versa. Cristina Henriquez, a third-generation member of the Henriquez Group of El Salvador, explains how this is done in her family:

> **As a business we (they) never really developed a core activity but rather always had a portfolio of different investments. … Usually the question of succession in a family business is dealt with by asking whether the next generation is interested in the family's activities. Mario Henriquez (the founder) was certainly not discouraged by the fact that his sons' passions rested in sectors other than retail. He knew how to convince them to join the family firm. "He just made it happen," declares Cristina. "My uncle, Luis, was interested in banking so my grandfather bought shares in a bank. My father was passionate about coffee and agriculture so my grandfather purchased a farm. His motto being to keep it in the family."[19]**

But for this to happen, members of the next generation must be able to listen not only to others but to their deepest thoughts as well, so they can know what they are really interested in. Nevertheless, thinking and listening to oneself is hard. Henry Ford called it "the hardest work there is, which is probably the reason why so few engage in it."

Today, a Hollywood Walk of Fame star has the name of celebrated comedian Steve Harvey. This is a far cry from his early life with a coal miner father and a mother who worked in a school cafeteria. As he reflects on his career trajectory, including stints as a mailman, a carpet cleaner, an insurance salesman, and a boxer, he talks about the importance of identifying one's gift:

> **Our creator, in his infinite wisdom, created every single soul with a gift. Your gift may be totally unique or it may be similar to someone else's, but know that your gift is *yours.*" When we utilize our gift, the universe thanks us by giving us an abundance of riches—from abundant opportunities to good health to financial wealth … Incorporating your gift into your life and sharing it with others will bring you joy, passion, and a new vigor for living life to the fullest.**[20]

As Harvey's winding career path shows, discovering one's "gift" can take a long time. One good way to understand this passion is to pay attention to what triggers one's curiosity. When asked what energizes him to take on new initiatives at age eighty-three, Rupert Murdoch, who transformed his father's news business into a global media conglomerate, remarked:

> **I am a permanently curious person. I probably waste my time being curious about things that have nothing to do with the business sometimes. What keeps me alive, certainly, is curiosity.**[21]

Walt Disney observed, "We keep moving forward, opening new doors, and doing new things, because we're curious and curiosity keeps leading us down new paths."[22] Perhaps Eleanor Roosevelt best captured the matchless importance of curiosity when she said:

> **I think, at a child's birth, if a mother could ask a fairy godmother to endow it with the most useful gift, that gift should be curiosity.**[23]

Curiosity is the desire to know more, learn more. It is triggered by things that surprise us because they do not conform to the norm[24] or because there could be multiple reasons for an occurrence. Psychologists have also found that we are least curious when we don't know anything at all about the topic—we simply don't know what to ask or think. Similarly, our curiosity also wanes when we know a lot about a topic because we have already asked all related questions that could have been asked. In other words, knowing a little triggers the desire to know more.

Enterprising families promote the cultivation of curious minds by exposing family and nonfamily members to different ideas and experiences through travel, conferences, or visits to other family enterprises. Perhaps the easiest way for such exposure is through reading or by watching movies, documentaries, or thoughtful commentaries on different topics. Access to these sources of new ideas has become significantly easier with the availability of electronic and recorded books, Ted Talks, and other media. Voracious readers not only broaden their own perspective and gain a deeper appreciation of themselves and their surroundings, but they also enrich their conversational repertoire. They use others' experiences and thoughts to broaden their cognitive horizons and learn the nuances of developing different skills necessary for entrepreneurial leadership. It is no surprise that some of the most successful entrepreneurs like Bill Gates, Warren Buffet, and Oprah Winfrey are well known for their avid reading habits. The younger generation of entrepreneurial leaders are not only reading themselves but take pride in recommending books to others.[25] For example, as his 2015 resolution Mark Zuckerberg, the founder and CEO of Facebook, not only vowed to read a book every two weeks, he invited people around the world to join him. There is no reason to be disappointed if some members of your family have not yet discovered what they are truly interested in or curious about. The only way they can find this out is through continuous exposure to new ideas and experiences.

Disciplined thinking not only helps in the identification of core interests of members of an enterprising family, but it also helps in decision making when conflicting values and priorities must be considered. It is in these less scripted parts and uncharted territories that entrepreneurial opportunities are more likely to exist. According to Harvard researchers Ikujiuro Nonaka and Hirotaka Takeuchi, wise leaders[26] relentlessly practice mind-stretching routines aimed to get to the core of the problem or situation. They construct and test alternate hypotheses by combining variables in unknown and untested ways to develop new solutions. Some individuals find solitude helps them to practice such mind-stretching routines, while others do them best while walking, cooking, gardening, dancing, hiking, swimming, or doing other activities. And some people need to engage in deep exploratory conversation with a supportive, non-judgmental person to think deeply.

Enterprising families realize that although listening, observing, and asking can seed different ideas in the mind, reflecting and thinking help to combine these ideas in unique ways to produce new combinations and ideas that entrepreneurial leaders of each generation can act upon to make a unique mark on their family enterprise.

Learning by Working

The overlap between family and business systems distinguishes family enterprises from all other organizational forms. Work easily seeps into the family domain, and vice versa. Just as next-generation family members often find themselves within earshot of business-related conversations, similarly those serious about getting some work experience can find opportunities with relative ease. Enterprising families find creative ways to engage the next generation at a young age. For example, at age thirteen, Scenic Root was able to get her work desk set up in the office of her grandmother's secretary. Perhaps this might be easier for a fifth-generation descendant of C. J. Root, who designed and manufactured the original Coca-Cola bottle.[27] But every next-generation member can find a few practical ways to get an exposure to their family business. Bill Rumpke Jr., for example, a second-generation family member and now the chief operating officer of Rumpke Waste and Recycling company,[28] insists that while the younger people in his family were not pressured to join the family business, interested juniors could get a job in the company sweeping floors even in grades six or seven, and they could ride the trucks with their fathers at an even younger age. As they grew older, if they expressed a keen interest in working they could get a truck from the company and the right to represent Rumpke in a certain area. They had to share part of the revenues generated from garbage collection with the company but got to keep the remainder for themselves. Not only did this motivate them to work harder, but it also taught them the value of money and how to deal with customers. While each route owner started by driving one truck and hauling garbage himself, over time as he picked up new customers, he could hire a driver and get a second truck, thereby growing the business by starting something new (route) and learning to manage or lead an employee.

It is in these less scripted parts and uncharted territories that entrepreneurial opportunities are more likely to exist.

Regardless of whether members of the next generation eventually end up working within or beyond their family enterprise, such learning experiences are great opportunities to learn and build skills. It is easier to start getting work experience with smaller part-time jobs within the family business than getting outside employment. Parents and grandparents are often more comfortable with having the next-generation members work on a part-time basis in the company at a young age while still in school. Enterprising families make sure to pay market wages to all their employees, including the next-generation family members, to differentiate their role as the child or grandchild of the controlling family from their role as an employee. Often, nonfamily members serve as the immediate superiors of juniors. This helps next-generation members to build a work ethic, earn some money, understand the business at its core, get to know the employees, and learn how different parts of the business connect with the overall organization. It also signals to family and nonfamily members alike that

Enterprising families make sure to pay market wages to all their employees, including the next-generation family members, to differentiate their role as the child or grandchild of the controlling family from their role as an employee.

the next generation is not afraid of hard work. Care is taken to treat the junior family member like any other employee, providing quality feedback and guidance.

In the most progressive families, seniors and juniors work together to develop a career plan to build the entrepreneurial leadership skills of each family member. Some next-generation members find it extremely helpful to work closely with their seniors who know the business. For example, Bill Berkeley, the great-grandson of the founder of the Tension Envelope Corporation established in 1886, worked his way up the sales ladder. Commenting on the seven years that he spent working full time for the company before becoming a CEO, he notes that it did not hurt to have two great mentors in his father and cousin.

"One of the great things was to learn from the ground up from people who had been there for a while," he states, adding, **"our sales and production are closely intertwined, and it was important to know both segments to get a broad view of the organization ... I needed to know the business firsthand to truly understand it and to have credibility with our associates."**[29]

Other members of the next generation believe they can learn better if they don't have to carry the additional baggage that comes with being the owners' son or daughter. "Get out there and grow" was the prevailing belief for James Fernley, a fifth-generation member of

Fernley & Fernley Inc., an association management company founded in 1886. Although since age five he knew that he wanted to be part of his family business, after graduating from university he worked for a competitor "to understand business from another perspective."[30] Members of his senior generation encouraged such work. Similarly, Jeremy Jacobs, the second-generation family member and chairman of Delaware North—a three-billion-dollar sports and entertainment company best known for TD Garden, the home of the Boston Bruins, made sure each of his three sons worked outside the company. Jerry Jacobs reported that when he and his brothers graduated from college, their father asked them to find their own jobs, as he wanted them to know what it was like to get and hold a job before coming to work for their family business. When they did join the family company, each had to work in a range of jobs in different divisions. When Jeremy relinquished the CEO title, the three brothers had long working experience outside and within the family company that had fully prepared them to take on the co-leadership roles.[31]

Learning by Creating

Next-generation family members have many opportunities to watch and talk to entrepreneurs within their familial networks. Some of them may have started new ventures, expanded the product or service lines, or taken their enterprise into new markets. Such proximity helps to build confidence to take on entrepreneurial activities.[32] But the story of success is mixed. While some next-generation family members do extremely well in building on the work of previous generations or starting new entrepreneurial ventures outside their family business, others face failures and frustrations. The distinguishing factor is the ability to augment others' experiences with one's own. The only ones who thrive are those who supplement learning by observing and listening with learning by doing. The type of doing we discussed earlier is largely focused on building the leadership skills by understanding the workings of an existing company. By experiencing work life in a follower's role and watching others give directions, juniors understand the feelings and motivations of employees in such positions. And over time, next-generation members may grow into supervisory or managerial positions, thus getting opportunities to practice delegation and getting work done through others. In this section, however, we focus on building entrepreneurial skills by creating something new.

To create something new, first one needs to come up with ideas. One of the ways to develop the skill of identifying opportunities for new products or services is by practicing on everyday experiences. Gary Green was working for his father's real estate business in New York when he felt frustrated with the cleaning services companies that overcharged landlords and tenants while providing mediocre services. He believed that the business model of the commercial cleaning services, where workers were on contract, needed to be changed to an employee-based model that provided fair salaries and benefits to ensure motivation, reliability, and continuity of quality services. In 1992 he started his venture, First Quality Management, to provide cleaning services to the properties owned by his family, enabling significant savings for the company and improving the services. With continuous hard work and refinement of his new model, by 2004 his company was providing cleaning services to over 100 buildings. Over time, the company added services such as security, messenger, restoration, and painting and also changed its name to Alliance Building Services. Reflecting on his decision to launch a cleaning service business independently from his family's real estate business, he notes that entrepreneurial ideas are born where "frustration meets execution." That is, when one person finds something frustrating, quite possibly many others feel the same. So, finding solutions to everyday frustrations leads to new business opportunities. For example, think about the last few times you traveled anywhere. What aggravations could have been resolved with a new product or service? How about the last time that you ate out or went shopping or to a film, concert, or sporting event? What would have made that a better experience? Once people develop the habit of thinking this way, they see new possibilities emerging everywhere.

When it comes to new creation, a bias for action is needed, as evidenced by the experiences of entrepreneurial startups like Starbucks, Staples, Costco, and others that Lloyd Shefsky documents in *Invent, Reinvent, & Thrive*.[33] An action orientation calls for just enough thinking about solutions to devise something that can actually be tried so as to get quick feedback from the users. It is also helpful to know what one can afford or is willing to lose—money, status, face, time—before giving up and trying something else. This is quite different from the "ready, aim, aim, aim, maybe fire" mind-set that some individuals may be inclined to take, spending enormous time to develop the presumably perfect foolproof plan[34] that never gets off the ground.

Stories of successful entrepreneurs are often sprinkled with a liberal dusting of small new initiatives since childhood. Examples may include small community projects like a lemonade stand or bake sale; or online sales and services or exchange of sports clothing or equipment, greeting or sports cards; or service ventures such as snow removal,

In the most progressive families, seniors and juniors work together to develop a career plan to build the entrepreneurial leadership skills of each family member.

gardening, dog walking, babysitting, or shopping for seniors. In any of these initiatives, there is a need to identify, acquire, and effectively use the human and financial resources needed to achieve an objective while creating something new that adds value to customers or clients. Adjustments will have to be made to ensure value is created and some unmet needs attended to. For next-generation members, such initiatives can focus on family or business. For example, in their quest to learn more about their family, particularly the extended family, some next-generation members of enterprising families take on a new project to document their genealogy or history. We have seen family members build strong networks by starting a family website that includes sections on family history, legacy, photographs, even YouTube videos. With the ease of availability of instruction and software programs to build genograms or family trees or history or websites, such projects are not only interesting, they also position the next-generation member in a desirable network node, while practicing entrepreneurial skills of starting something new and worthwhile. Over time, one can graduate from simpler ideas to more complex ones.

> *The only ones who thrive are those*
> *who supplement learning by observing and*
> *listening with learning by doing.*

At times, siblings or cousins may band together to co-create new initiatives under the rubric of their family business. For example, six eighteen- to thirty-five-year old cousins of the fourth generation of Australia's Brown Brothers worked together, secretly from their parents and grandparents, to develop and launch two distinctive wine blends under a new brand, Kid You Not. While this renowned family-owned wine company has been known for its traditional wines since 1889, with a history going as far back as 1860, the new wines developed by juniors aimed to meet the needs of their age group.[35] They had a lot of fun developing their concept and implementing their ideas, while getting to know each other in a uniquely intimate yet professional manner. Developing their entrepreneurial skills together enhanced their understanding of each other and enabled them to gain the respect of their senior family members as well as nonfamily executives.

Engaging Personal Advisors

In addition to continuous learning, enterprising family members often virtually create a "Personal Advisory Board" that is committed to their growth and guidance. Experienced family or nonfamily members may be placed in such advisory positions for juniors. Senior family members—whether in or out of the business—who can understand different points of views prevalent in the family, friends, peers, faculty members from school, or professional peers from industry associations are some good sources of advisors. The best advisors are those who ask great questions that help the family member to reflect on possibilities, can anticipate potential trouble spots, are good at thinking up alternative methods of solving problems, and care enough about the individual to deliver hard messages when necessary. While such advisors need not come together for regular meetings, as is the case with boards in general, it is important to be in touch with them regularly so they can serve as sounding boards. Gary Green had Richard Branson, Warren Buffet, and his dad serve as advisors. In a lecture at his alma mater, the University of Vermont, he mentioned that he makes sure to meet with his advisors at least six times a year and encouraged the students to do the same with their trusted advisors. Advisors may change over time as life evolves and need not be famous to be helpful.

To illustrate how personal advisors can play a role in helping resolve the dilemmas of members of the next generation, we share a recent experience we had with a young Latina whom we met during her senior year at Babson College while planning a conference. "Rita Marquez"[36] did a superb job in this conference, gaining our high respect. After graduation, she was working in her family business and got very concerned about the unfolding dynamics among the family involved in the business. This included her parents (founders), brother (now CEO), and two sisters (one VP of sales living in the United States and one CEO of a division). Rita, youngest of the siblings, was herself the CEO of another division in another Central American country, a stretch job for her since she was a recent graduate and the youngest in the business. She reached out to us for advice, which we were eager to provide given the regard we had for her. Here's how she described the problem:

All my brothers and sisters involved in the family business will be in [our home country] this weekend. Thus, I wanted to use this opportunity to have a family meeting as there have been many unresolved problems that need to be fixed. However,

I need advice in how to guide the process in order to make it a proactive session instead of a session where feelings will be hurt.

We asked her to provide some more details about her family, the business, and their current dilemma. Here is what she shared with us:

- My family never talks about problems; people don't like to openly talk about their feelings.
- In December 2011, my dad transferred the baton as CEO to my brother. This decision had the support of all family members.
- My dad transferred the baton as we were pressuring him to pass it on. We were getting quotes from consultants. However, he did it without a consultant. Without telling anyone in the company, in his speech at the Christmas dinner he passed the baton over to my brother "Hector."
- My brother has implemented new projects that have allowed the company to maintain sustained growth in a very rough economy.
- My father remained in the company as legal advisor/supervising stores/public relations.
- In 2013, Hector was diagnosed with very delicate health issues.
- Hector is actively involved with many charitable organizations (as chapter president in some cases). This has forced my mother and my father to get more involved in the business and the power has changed again towards the founders.
- Currently my mother's and my dad's health have declined due to stress and pressure. They complain about my brother's absence and the workload they are carrying, as he is not focusing on the business, as he should.
- On the other hand, my brother complains about my parents doing things without his consent.

I have called a three-hour family meeting on Sunday. I need to create a dynamic that will allow me to reveal these problems without talking about it directly. I need to trust the process, but

I have no idea what dynamic to create. Or how to go about it? HELP SOS.

A long telephone conversation with Rita was enough to help her think through the way she wanted to approach the meeting and bolster her confidence to proceed. The challenge of getting things on the table without talking about it directly sounds almost impossible (although not terribly unusual), yet she reported great progress. Here is the agenda she created (only indirectly based on any advice she got from us):

Agenda:
1. **Life Box:** Where are people at in their life? Where do they want to go? Are you happy where you are?

2. **Business Box:** What are we giving in the business? What does the business need from each one of us?

3. Possible scenarios?

4. What are our takeaways?

With a few rules:
1. No cellphones

2. If someone gives his or her opinion, you can't answer with your point of view. First you must ask three questions.

3. No interruptions

Rita reported the following positive agreements coming out of the meeting:

1. **Quantitative evaluations for family members (a completely new idea, embraced by all).**

   a. Board meetings for Division 1 (even months)

   b. Board meetings for Division 2 (odd months)

2. **We must be headhunters.**

   a. Creation of an in-company program that allows employees to grow inside the company (star project)

   b. Developing managers who are leaders

   c. Evaluations of all managers

   d. Internship program (structured, paid)

3. **Be in continuous improvement.**

   a. Intradepartmental Quality Circles

4. **Boosting growth in private label for the two major product areas.**

Three months later Rita reported:

Last week, we had our first board meeting after the intervention. All the family members presented their quantitative evaluations. I think it was a great start because it helped us to focus on the priorities the company is expecting of us, and we could see the improvements immediately. From this experience I would encourage all family businesses to be more quantitative with their family members' evaluations, and actually have evaluations.

A recent update from Rita was even more encouraging. The overall business was thriving, and she personally was growing and doing very well.

Such positive results are definitely not guaranteed every time, and we have to acknowledge that this enterprising family is remarkable for moving rapidly to a way of creating objective data that would enable more authentic conversation. And they are remarkable not only for allowing a recent graduate to be the CEO of a small division as a stretch learning experience but also being for being willing to follow her lead in this family meeting. But we offer it as an example of how asking someone who is trusted for advice can be very useful, even if the specific advice is not exactly followed. Talking about it, asking questions, and listening to the reactions can help anyone sort out the tangled emotions and come up with an action plan that fits the family's culture.

Part of how the next-generation members can build entrepreneurial leadership skills, including how to create a vision, get people aligned behind it, manage the trade-offs among diverse points of view and between risk and reward, short-term and long-term, is by doing it. Rita Marquez in the previous example is doing exactly that by managing a new, small division in another country, being stretched all the time. And when she felt that her family could be getting itself into a conundrum, knowing our experiences with family enterprises, she was quick to reach out to us. Based on our discussions, she was able to lead the first family meeting for their family and get it on a positive track.

Some next-generation members may fall into the fundamental attribution error of blaming the situation. Instead of taking the initiative to build their entrepreneurial leadership skills, they may convince themselves that their parents don't allow them to do this or that their family business is not set up to do that. But the most enterprising ones create appropriate learning challenges out of any assignment they are working on. Remember Henry Ford's remark: "Whether you think you can, or think you can't, you are probably right." The son of a farmer from Dearborn, Michigan, although Ford did not invent the automobile or the assembly line, through persistent trial-and-error he was able to shape transportation and manufacturing in the twentieth century. Following the mantra of not finding faults but remedies instead, he persevered to find solutions that worked. As a young boy he organized other boys to build rudimentary steam engines and water

The next-generation members can build entrepreneurial leadership skills, including how to create a vision, get people aligned behind it, manage the trade-offs among diverse points of view, between risk and reward, short-term and long-term ... by doing it.

wheels—an early form of leading others. As he got older he took on demanding and perhaps undesirable jobs such as working as a night engineer at the Edison Electric Illuminating Company—not because he knew much about electricity but he saw it as an opportunity to learn new skills. Over time, he became good friends with his role model, Thomas Edison. Being fired from his first job and failing in the first two companies he formed, in hindsight, seem to have added to building his entrepreneurial leadership skills. You can too!

Using the following work sheet for yourself or other family members, assess strengths related to each of the five forms of learning discussed in this chapter, and identify some things to work and improve upon. Develop a meaningful, measurable action plan so that the practice of building entrepreneurial skills can be part of your routine.

WORK SHEET 2

Assessment and Action Plan to Develop Entrepreneurial

Leadership Skills of _____ (name)

	Things _____ does well	Things _____ can do better
Learning by absorbing		
Learning by interacting		
Learning by reflecting		
Learning by working		
Learning by creating		

Action Plan: Develop a measurable action plan of what

_____ would like to accomplish:

Time Frame	Target Goals	Practical Practice Items

Chapter 3

SECRETS OF SUCCESSFUL
ENTERPRISING FAMILIES

In 1745 Johann Diederich Neuhaus (JDN) built his first wooden shaft winch for the locks and the horse-drawn barges on the Ruhr river in Witten, Germany. Could he have known that in the vicinity of his family home he had laid the foundation of a company that would become a world leader in effortless movement of heavy loads? Seven generations after its foundation, JDN, led by Wilfried Neuhaus-Galladé, is one of the forty-four Henokien[1] companies. (To become a member of the Henokien association, a company must have been in existence for over 200 years and be actively controlled and managed by the founders' descendants.) Over the years, the winch forge has been transformed into a globally operating specialist for pneumatic and hydraulic hoists. While adapting to the changing market needs, each generation of this enterprising family has added a unique layer of entrepreneurial contributions to build on the work of previous generations. Today, JDN produces over 8,000 hoists a year for seventy industries across ninety countries. Meeting complex safety standards, its products work effectively in conditions ranging from icy to extreme heat.

Over its 270-year history, the Neuhaus family has had its share of highs and lows, as they enjoyed growing their enterprise to a world leadership position in their industry, while persevering through deaths, wars, and the political turmoil of Germany. As an example, third-generation member Johann Diederich II had sent his most talented son Carl to a well-regarded engineering academy with hopes that he could regenerate the company. But Lieutenant Carl Neuhaus died in the war of 1870. Another son died before he could become a winch master, leaving the third son, Louis Neuhaus to carry the company forward, which he did with all his energy. But, once again, death struck this family as Louis died at fifty-seven. The company could easily have closed down if his wife Emma had not stepped forward to take the responsibility of running the business. Although she had no experience in the industry or in working with an unskilled labor force, she relied on hard work and a trusted nonfamily foreman who had learned his trade in the Neuhaus smithy to keep the company afloat, until her nineteen-year-old son Max was ready to take over the business.

For a family business to prevail over time, two conditions must be met. First, the family must persist, and second, the business must continue.[2] For the latter to happen, the products and services offered must continue to evolve to meet the needs of changing markets. Thus its organization must be well equipped to nurture entrepreneurship at all levels. The JDN products evolved from winches for the locks and horse-drawn barges on the Ruhr river in 1745, to those capable of moving loads of up to 7,500 kg in coal mines around 1880, to ones lifting rail carriages onto the tracks by 1925. Today, using air and pneumatic hoists and cranes, their products can move loads of up to 100 tons (100,000 kg) safely in industries such as oil and gas exploration, heavy plant construction, and mining.

A meaningful involvement of the controlling family in business is critical for its continuity as a family business. The Zildjian Company shows the dual importance of both the family name and the continuous involvement of the family in a firm. In 1623, Avedis Zildjian started his cymbal foundry in the Constantinople region. In 1929, direct descendants of Avedis set up the first Zildjian cymbal foundry in America. Since 1999, fourteenth-generation members, sisters Craigie and Debbie Zildjian, are at the helm of this enterprising family business as their next generation prepares to make its entrepreneurial contributions. Continuity of family involvement and the name of the firm enable this family to trace and celebrate its historical roots.

The level of flexibility and adaptation evident in this company has persisted through the untimely deaths of family members, the move across the Atlantic, wars, fires, political turmoil, and the Great Depression, and has led it to invent new models of cymbals for use in religious feasts, prayers, royal weddings, military bands, and symphonies—all while sticking together as the Zildjian cymbal family. This suggests that both the continuity of a firm's name and the family involvement in the enterprise are necessary conditions for the longevity of a family firm. Let's pause to capture some of the basics about your family and its enterprise.

Work Sheet 3

Our Family and Its Enterprise(s)

I. How is your family capturing its historical roots and evolution?

---

2. How far back can you trace the enterprise(s) of your family?

3. What is your definition of a family?

4. Starting from the most senior generation for which you have the information (call it G1), list the number of siblings and cousins in each generation:

Generation Number	Number of Siblings and Cousins	Average # of Children per Sibling/Cousin
G1		
G2		
G3		
..		
Your Generation		

5. How many generations of your family are currently working full-time anywhere? How many in your family enterprise/s? What is the age of the oldest and youngest member of your family working full time?

Number of generations working full-time anywhere: _____

Number of generations working in your family enterprises: _____

Age of the oldest member of your family working full-time: _____

Age of the youngest member of your family working full-time: _____

Based on your answers to the above questions, how would you describe your family's structure over time?

What Is a Family?

The family is one of the most enduring units of human organization biologically, socially, and economically. Family scientists note the nature of families to change and adapt over time and place.[3] Its tenacity as a unit of organization has been credited to its ability to transform itself over time. The family economist and Nobel laureate Gary Becker notes that families persist because they are highly efficient at adapting to societal needs.[4] For example, in the last century, mirroring the dominant forms of economic activity—pre-industrial, industrial, post-industrial—family structures have changed from extended multigenerational, to nuclear, to the heterogeneous family structures of today that satisfy diversity and fluid movement of society.

Family structure has profound implications for the longevity of family enterprises. With longer life spans and fewer children in each generation, many families of today have a long and narrow *beanpole*[5] structure. For the first time in human history, there is a *multigenerational stack up* as four generations are often in the work place simultaneously.[6] With longer, healthier lives and advances in medicine and technology, humans can work longer. For members of the younger generation, with the plethora of educational and life choices, the start of full-time work and family life is often delayed to the thirties as they work their way through the choices to discover their true passions and interests. But there seems to be no hurry either, as the family enterprise appears to be in very good hands with members of the senior generations solidly in charge and often in no rush to let go of their role given that they enjoy productive, healthy lives and careers. Although the actual time when the next generation may be needed to take over the leadership of the current enterprise may be delayed by a decade or even two perhaps, what happens when the time comes and no family member is available, ready, or eager to take charge? In some families, next-generation members may not have the desire or patience to wait twenty to thirty years for the top job in their family enterprise. In others, they may have no interest in the industry sector or location in which their family business operates. Alternatively, what if too many siblings or cousins feel they are ready for the top jobs? Whose perspective must count when it comes to determining the readiness of next-generation members to take charge of a unit or the enterprise? There are often multiple and quite disparate perspectives on this issue within the same family.[7]

Enterprising families that thrive over generations tend to be less rigid and more inclusive when they make decisions not only on who are considered part of their family but also on which family members can contribute to the enterprise. Such families tend to focus on the essence or behaviors rather than on factors such as blood relationship, marital status, gender, birth order, cohabitation, and similar factors when they decide which family members can contribute to the enterprise. Their concept of family may be a more flexible one, where path dependence, aspirations, and behaviors mark the in- and out-group:

Family is a group of people affiliated through bonds of shared history and a commitment to share a future together while supporting the development and well-being of individual members.[8]

They often do not follow restrictive definitions, such as these:

Family is a group of persons related to one another by blood or marriage; or
Family is a group of parents and children living together in a household.

Of course, there is no *one* right way to define family. But it is worth reflecting on the profound practical implications of different definitions for enterprising families. Most of us don't discuss our definition of family. Unconsciously, however, each of us absorbs the familial norms and acceptable modes of behavior from previous generations. We then combine these with our own experiences and observations to develop a concept of family that we often consider the "right" one. Unstated assumptions about who falls within or outside the family's boundary often creep up in business families when they discuss family involvement in the business or dividing up the family's assets. At times, only such sensitive conversations make different members of family realize that all members are not aligned in their basic conception of family and, more importantly, in the nature and degree of its involvement in the business.

Societal values regarding gender roles, generational hierarchy, and the institution of marriage are currently undergoing significant changes. The norms from just a few decades ago are being challenged and stretched in multiple directions.[9] Overall, the push is towards more inclusion, diversity, and leveling of the ground for members of different genders, generations, races, and religions. Amidst such changes, it would be more remarkable if *all* family members shared the same concept of family or its nature of engagement in business. Different perspectives are more likely. Some family members draw the boundary at blood relatives when it comes to involvement in the ownership, management, or governance of the business. Such rigid, clearly demarcated definitions can be helpful for making decisions. Nevertheless, such thinking limits the pool of possible leaders of their business, as it leaves little room for in-laws or adopted family members or nonfamily members to contribute to the enterprise through these significant roles. Other families follow the more constraining norm of primogeniture and restrict the leadership of the enterprise to the eldest son. In this case, the younger sons and daughters are not considered for leadership roles. Of course, all efforts can then be directed to nurture the entrepreneurial leadership abilities of this preordained successor. At times, such additional attention is highly successful. In addition, a clear statement about who the next leader will be can minimize confusion among siblings or cousins and avoid misunderstandings. But what happens when this chosen one is not interested in or is not the most—or at all—capable to run the enterprise?

The centuries-old Japanese *mukoyōshi* practice carefully selects and legally adopts adult males to fulfill the offspring role and lead the family enterprise when needed. This practice is perhaps the most extreme case known of defining the family based on the behavior or essence of a person. Well-recognized family firms—such as Canon, Kikkoman, Suzuki, and Toyota—have all utilized this strategy at some point in their history. Other variations of this strategy, such as passing the leadership role to a son- or daughter-in-law, have prevailed for centuries and continue in business enterprises around the world. In fact, it is currently being considered by the oldest family business in the world—the Houshi Ryokan, a traditional Japanese inn that can trace its history over 1,300 years. It first opened its doors in 718 and has been passed down over forty-six generations.

In some instances, the evolution in fundamental concepts, such as which family members can lead the business, happens due to circumstances. In JDN, for example, although the family originally did not envision female in-laws running the enterprise, untimely deaths of the fourth-generation Neuhaus men propelled Emma, an in-law, into the leadership role. Even when death or incapacitation is not involved, leaders of progressive enterprising families remain steadfast in appointing the best candidates to the jobs. For example, Laurent Beaudoin succeeded his father-in-law, Joseph Armand Bombardier, who founded the Canadian aerospace and transportation giant in 1937. Today, this company has a nonfamily CEO, while Laurent's son serves as the chairman of the board reinforcing the inclusive engagement of family and nonfamily in this enterprise, which prefers to place the most suitable person in each key role. In Walmart, another large family-controlled company, Greg Penner, the grandson-in-law of founder Sam Walton, took over as the chairman of the board from his father-in-law Rob Walton in 2015.[10] A family business thought leader and advisor, John Davis, illustrates using examples from Cargill, Hermes, McIlhenny, and Ford that family or nonfamily members, whether from within a family enterprise or outside it, can be an effective CEO under different conditions. Successful leaders balance continuity of core values with needed changes in activities and practices.[11]

Not only are sons-in-law getting more involved in major leadership positions of family enterprises, but the presence of female leaders from the next generation suggests that the gender playing field has been leveled in progressive family enterprises around the world. Examples include Abigail Johnson at Fidelity Investments of the United States, Preetha Reddy at Apollo Hospitals of India, Winnie Chu at Dorsett Hospitality of Hong Kong, Delphine Arnault at France's Louis Vuitton, and Mona Yousuf Almoayyed at Y. K. Almoayyed & Sons of Bahrain, to name just a few. Enterprising families focus on expanding the horizons and skill sets of all family members of the next generation to expand their pool of talented leaders from within the family and beyond.[12]

Increasing flexibility and transitioning to a new conception of family can take a toll, however. In the case of Houshi Ryokan, the oldest son of the forty-seventh generation died prematurely. He had been expected to own the company and handle the family's responsibility of protecting the inn and hot springs for the future generations. His death left his younger sister as the only member of his generation. She is a university graduate who was working as a doctor's secretary and had ambitions of teaching and helping other people. After her brother's untimely death, the responsibility of the inn has fallen upon her. The burden and stress on both generations is evident from the following comments in a video interview with the family:

> **Wife of the forty-sixth-generation family leader: "It has been fifty years since I got married to my husband. I hadn't met my husband until our marriage was arranged. For my children, looking at it in a modern way, they should choose freely and not have an arranged marriage. Even if it's arranged, it's not guaranteed they'd be in love. So they don't have to get married this way. I would like them to have a romantic relationship."**
>
> **Daughter who is the only surviving family member of the forty-seventh generation: "I was looking for a partner and I was thinking to move away when I got married. But now my parents only introduce me to men who can be adopted into the Houshi family. What my parents are thinking is not the same as me, so that's confusing me. ... We are confused and worried because we don't know who the 47th owner will be. ... There were times I had wished that I hadn't been born as a member of the Houshi."**
>
> **The forty-sixth-generation owner of the Houshi family: "The Houshi family's responsibilities are to pass our long history for future generations and protect our hot spring. ... My daughter hasn't gotten married yet. ... (She) is the right person to do it. ... We will be waiting for her.**[13]

The challenges felt when transitioning to a new conception of family are not unique to Japan however. Curt Carlson founded the Carlson Company in 1914. He led the enterprise for sixty years and made it one of the largest privately held hospitality and travel enterprises in the world, with annual revenues of $8.1 billion. Curt Carlson was an old-school entrepreneur who felt the leadership position was a man's domain. He had no sons of his own, however. Despite his daughter Marilyn's interest in and aptitude for running the family business since she was young, only a year before he died at eighty-four in 1998 did he name her his successor. When he became ill in his seventies, Curt appointed his son-in-law as CEO for a brief period, only to reclaim the leadership once he recovered. Did this interim appointment of his son-in-law as CEO signal his struggle to renegotiate the concept of family and gender roles that he had grown up with? A student of family business, Curt eventually named his daughter as his successor, while also creating a nine-member board, with three members elected by each of the two daughters and another three independents. In 2013, Diana Nelson, a third-generation member of the Carlson family, took over the role of board Chair from her mother, who held the job for ten years after the founder died. While these leadership transitions appear seamless now, there were some challenging moments for the incumbent leaders in making these decisions. Curt expected Marilyn's son and his namesake, Curtis Carlson Nelson, to succeed his mother as a CEO. And Curtis did serve as the president and chief operating officer of the company for some time. But the board did not select him to lead the company, citing poor performance and substance abuse. Instead, his sister Diane was selected for the top job. Even for one of the most enterprising companies in the world, the family concepts of gender and blood relationships seem to be deeply rooted over generations. In her 2008 book, Marilyn expresses sadness in having to let go of her dream of passing the leadership of her father's business to her son.

Family Dualities

While there is no perfect definition of a family or the roles of each member in it, each choice opens some possibilities and limits others when it comes to developing entrepreneurs in every generation. In enterprising families, the following ambidexterities help create superior environments to develop the entrepreneurial skills of each generation:

- Core strength *and* flexibility
- My dreams *and* our shared dreams
- Warm acceptance *and* high expectations
- Learning from within *and* beyond
- Money sense *and* emotional sensibilities

Core Strength *and* Flexibility

Core strength and flexibility are deeply woven in the mind-set of long-lasting entrepreneurial families. This duality is found in both the family and the business systems. For example, while the institution of family is protected, the changes in its conception are embraced to reflect the societal values and the unique situational needs of the family. Boundaries separating in- and out-groups are not considered impermeable or drawn forever. Instead, they are reexamined as circumstances change over time. *Flexibility* is the sacrosanct core strength. The core institution of family is not left untended, however. Mindful efforts and investments of time and resources are made to instill family pride. The efforts undertaken to strengthen and nurture the familial bonds range from simple things such as spending time together, sharing family stories, and developing unique family traditions to resource-intensive initiatives such as producing commemorative histories and biographical videos or building museums or institutions in the family's name. As the family grows or shrinks in size, it takes new and innovative thinking to keep it cohesive and together. It is made clear to those within the family and to the world that their allegiance to their family is strong.[14] Symbolic and substantive gestures are used to reinforce such messaging, as in the simple tag line of "SC Johnson, a family company since 1886."

Jim Collins, the author of best sellers like *Built to Last* and *Good to Great*, has devoted a significant portion of his career to studying enduring human entities such as companies, nations, religions, and families. In a conversation with Bruce Feiler for his remarkable book *The Secrets of Happy Families*, Collins remarked that one common feature of enduring entities is their ability to "preserve the core / stimulate progress."[15] According to him, "Core is something so central you would say:

'Even if it's harmful to us, we would still hold on to this value. Even if we had to pay penalties, even if we had to punish our children for violating it, even if we had to deny them something that would bring them pleasure, we would still hold it.'" He cautions: "It is not what you think these values should be, but what they are. Only if they are deeply authentic can you hold on to them when it's inconvenient, and that's when you know it is core."

A vivid example of a company that made some significant decisions based on its Southern Baptist core beliefs is Chick-fil-A, an American fast-food chain from Georgia that specializes in chicken sandwiches. Founded in 1946 by S. Truett Cathy, since 2013 this family enterprise has been led by the founder's son, Daniel Truett, who is the chairman, president, and CEO. With over 1,900 locations and annual sales exceeding $6 billion, this family firm has enjoyed positive sales growth for forty-seven consecutive years while sticking close to its values, one of which is not to open any store on Sundays. Here is how the company explains its decision:

Why We're Closed on Sundays

Our founder, Truett Cathy, made the decision to close on Sundays in 1946 when he opened his first restaurant in Hapeville, Georgia. He has often shared that his decision was as much practical as spiritual. He believes that all franchised Chick-fil-A Operators and their restaurant employees should have an opportunity to rest, spend time with family and friends, and worship if they choose to do so. That's why all Chick-fil-A restaurants are closed on Sundays. It's part of our recipe for success.[16]

Of course, this specific value is important to the Cathy family, but the example illustrates how major decisions can be based on core values. Flexibility is demonstrated by the product and process innovations of the company, including the establishment of restaurants in shopping malls in 1967, and the variety of restaurant formats in use today, including stand-alone, drive-through, and full service. Product innovations continue with the latest addition of Hawaiian-inspired seafood items like mahi-mahi, Ahi tuna, cod, calamari, and shrimp, which are available alongside the traditional favorites—chicken sandwiches, waffle fries, and milkshakes.[17]

Families that run enduring enterprises and successfully nurture entrepreneurs in every generation make change and flexibility their core value, as evident in the following comments made by family members of later generations:

- There is no resting on what happened yesterday.[18] (Josh Johnson, fourth-generation president and an in-law of the Hudson family of Fidelitone Logistics, founded in 1929.)

- We continued to do things that were different, whether it was with the envelope or with the process.[19] (Dick Berkley, third-generation member of Tension Envelope Company, founded 1886. Even the family name was changed from Berkowitz to Berkley in 1941.)

- Our family's entrepreneurial instincts are in our DNA. Each generation has expressed [its] entrepreneurial instincts by developing new businesses. Elisha started with a woodenware company. Charles brought the family into the forest products industry. For Mowry Sr. it was the manufacture of corrugated boxes and the fortuitous acquisition of a plastics business. Tad acquired a variety of businesses yet his most enduring contribution was his management philosophy. The fifth-generation innovations are inside the business, at the board level, and at the family level.[20] (Sylvia Shepard, fifth-generation owner of Menasha Corporation, founded in 1850.)

In each of these cases, flexibility and change emerge as core values. They are shown not only in the conception of family and its involvement in the business, but also in different aspects of their enterprise. Each generation is expected to focus on continuous improvements and changes not only in terms of products, services, or markets, but also in terms of processes and governance of family and its enterprise. While there is clearly a pride in the past contributions, each generation feels its core responsibility is to ensure the enterprise remains relevant amidst the changing environment. The entrepreneurial

*A balance between individual dreams and the
shared dream is essential to the psychological
well-being of all family members as well as to the
harmony of the enterprise.*

---

mind-set compels family owners to take responsibility for finding new
ventures and revenue streams and, like an avid gardener, to prune and
abandon nonperforming assets. Evolution through regeneration and
creative destruction are natural forces in these enterprising families.

My Dreams *and* Our Shared Dreams

Shared family dreams reflect the fundamental values and aspirations
of a family—defining who they are and what their family name and
its enterprise stands for. Children of successful enterprising families
often struggle with the *individuation* process that helps to differentiate their unique selves from those of their family and its enterprise.
While all humans must distinguish their individual identity from that
of their parents, the process has been found to be stunted for those
born in the cradle of a successful family business. In his classic book
Succeeding Generations: Realizing the Dream of Families in Business,
Ivan Lansberg notes that next-generation family members

> are born into an intricate fabric already woven by the parents.
> As they grow, they must decide whether they can weave their
> individual dreams into the family pattern—or must untangle
> their threads from the tapestry and look for different patterns
> that seem more promising.
>
> To them, the family business is seldom a neutral entity; it is a
> force in shaping their sense of who they are and what they want
> in their lives. On the one hand, business can be a vehicle that

makes their dreams happen. On the other, it can be a barrier that blocks the fulfillment of their own dream.

They may choose to enter it enthusiastically, or they may wish to select entirely different careers. Whatever their choice, the business is likely to be a powerful influence on their developing ideas about themselves and the world. ...

A balance between individual dreams and the shared dream is essential to the psychological well-being of all family members as well as to the harmony of the enterprise. The ability to strike this balance requires a degree of individuation and personal maturity on the part of each family member.[21]

Ideas for new creations and innovations cannot emerge when a next-generation member is not wholly committed to a career path. Research has revealed at least four different reasons that motivate next-generation family members to take up a full-time career in their family enterprise. These are:

- Desire to contribute to the growth of the enterprise
- Feeling of obligation toward the family
- Concern for potential loss of inherited wealth if a full-time job is not pursued in the family enterprise
- Insecurity about finding a better job outside the family firm

The following quotes from next-generation family members, all of whom chose to pursue a full-time career in their family enterprise, illustrate these different motivations:

I'm one of the luckiest guys to come out of the university because I haven't been slotted into a specific job. We have an item that we manufacture from scratch, we warehouse it, we wholesale it, and we retail it. I see the business from every angle and I'm involved in it from every angle. It's kind of neat to be able to do that. ... I love being part of my family business. [desire to contribute]

I felt touched; I felt needed, but I felt uncertain that this (moving to the family business) was a good move. ... He (my father) said that the most important thing right now is for you as a (family member) to be visible here because your sister is out. .... [so] we need another family member here. And so with that kind of plea I had no choice in my mind. I couldn't let the family down. So I dropped everything I was doing and ... I just went the next day and started working. [obligation toward the family]

At that point we really didn't know what her (the wife's) involvement was from a shareholders' standpoint. And what we found out was she was heavily involved to the point where it dwarfed what we were doing personally and all of a sudden it did change our perspective. ... It sort of changed our outlook on it (their family business) ... that is when we decided we cannot pass this up. [potential loss of inherited wealth]

I was always afraid of change (working outside of family business). I'll stick it out ... I really think, in a way, being so cowardly. I've really been lucky; I've done as well as I have so far. ... It could have been a lot worse. [insecurity about finding a job][22]

Those who join because of desire have been found to be strong performers and effective entrepreneurial leaders of their family firms. One might expect that joining due to obligation would have a paralyzing effect on performance due to long-term resentment. Interestingly, research indicates minimal negative effect on leadership effectiveness or performance. On the other hand, those who are motivated because of the opportunity cost tend to be less effective. The least successful, however, are those for whom perceived need is the driving factor, as they experience the lowest levels of career success and are ineffective performers.[23] These findings reinforce that families must build mechanisms to develop and articulate the aspirations of each individual member and carve out a shared family dream.

Lansberg, who has helped hundreds of families to develop their shared dream, observes that "for a workable shared dream to emerge, the individual dreams of family members must overlap substantially; otherwise, there may not be enough common ground to build a satisfactory future scenario. ... Obviously, the broader the common ground, the greater the possibility for effective collaboration."[24] Next-generation family members may differ significantly in the ways their individual dreams and aspirations mesh with those of the family, and accordingly, vary in how much of their self they are willing to truly invest in the continuity or growth of their family enterprise. Recognizing these psychological factors at play, enterprising families that succeed in cultivating entrepreneurs in each generation are often willing to accept different aspirations in their children. One of the best examples of this is Warren Buffet, the chairman, CEO, and president of Berkshire Hathaway, one of the wealthiest, most influential, and most respected business magnates in the world. He is well known for not wanting to spoil his kids, and he encourages them to follow their passions and be the best they possibly can be by earnestly pursuing their talents. One son is a successful farmer, and the other is an Emmy award-winning musician. Peter Buffet, the musician son, once remarked that "his parents urged him to figure out his passion, and he dabbled with music but didn't think he was talented enough to take it seriously. At age nineteen, after three semesters at Stanford, two things happened: he decided to give music another chance, and he inherited a share of his grandfather's farm, which his father converted to $90,000 in Berkshire Hathaway stock. Today, that stock would be worth $120 million; instead, he dropped out of college and sold the stock to launch a music career—with his father's blessing." He started out doing background music for commercials on networks like MTV, produced a few New Age albums, did the score for the firedance scene in the movie *Dances With Wolves*, and composed the full score for *500 Nations*, the eight-hour Emmy-awarded CBS miniseries produced by Kevin Costner.[25] Earlier in his career, when he did not enjoy musical success, he fell behind on his mortgage payments but pulled through on his own without his parents bailing him out. In his words:

> I certainly wouldn't have the self-confidence or the self-worth if my parents were always there saying, "Let me help, let me help." ... My dad cared—both my parents did—but they weren't there to just swoop in and save the day. That was *huge*.
>
> The reason why my dad and I get along so well is because we never ask the other one to be something they're not. ... He allowed me to be me and not something I wasn't.[26]

Knowing and pursuing one's dream is as important and powerful as enabling other family members to pursue theirs. Entrepreneurial families that accept differences within family members are better positioned to articulate a shared dream for their family enterprise. Once this dream is clear, the mechanisms and pathways to accomplish it become a collective discussion. Entrepreneurial families have been found to take longer in making decisions about the directions of innovations to pursue, but once a decision is made, implementation is faster than their nonfamily counterparts.[27] This parallels high-performing teams, in which members commit to one another and to team performance in part because they also see that they can get their individual needs met.

Warm Acceptance *and* High Expectations

Families set the acceptable norms and standards for their next generation. Growing up, we know which behaviors will make our parents and grandparents proud and which will disappoint them. While there is warm acceptance and understanding that different family members will have unique passions and dreams and be endowed with their own strengths and talents, how far each is pushed along these directions varies significantly in families. In some cases, mediocre performance is considered acceptable, but the most progressive entrepreneurial families encourage excellence. According to Peter Buffet, while his parents supported his passion for music, their guidance was to become the best he possibly could if he followed this pursuit. In this duality of warm acceptance and high expectations, each member of the family enjoys the freedom to distinguish his or her self from other family members without carrying the burden of inter-sibling comparisons. Stretch goals are part of everyday norms in such families. When interviewed by the Women Corporate Directors, Marilyn Carlson Nelson, who led her family enterprise Carlson Company for ten years after her father retired, noted how he imbued the desire to excel in her by pushing her to "strive for an A rather than A-; to run for president rather than vice-president."[28]

Research on personality traits has revealed that entrepreneurs score higher than non-entrepreneurs in *openness to experiences*.[29] Enterprising families find ways to inculcate a desire to learn while

*Knowing and pursuing one's dream is as
important and powerful as enabling other family
members to pursue theirs. Entrepreneurial
families that accept differences within family
members are better positioned to articulate a
shared dream for their family enterprise.*

doing something different into the mind-set of family members at a young age. At age twelve, when Marilyn Carlson Nelson announced to her parents that she no longer wanted to attend Sunday school because of its dull curriculum, her father insisted, "If you don't like it, fix it!," and asked her to make a list of ways to fix it. Later, her mother drove her to the Sunday school superintendent to whom she was to present her concerns and ideas. Taking her seriously, the superintendent formed a group of students which he asked her to lead to fix the program.[30] The effect of this learning moment was so profound for her that when she was interviewed after her ten years at the helm of one of the largest hospitality companies in the world, she recounted it as one of the important learning moments of her life.[31] Her father had challenged her to think of ways to improve the Sunday school rather than turning a blind eye on the problem, thus encouraging her to think of new solutions to identified problems. By asking her to present her thoughts to the superintendent, her parents set in motion an opportunity to learn to articulate her ideas, work in a team, and take responsibility for making a meaningful difference in her community—all without them providing the solutions directly. Instead, they used the moment to let her experience the entrepreneurial learning.

Learning from Within *and* Beyond

Next-generation members of long-lasting entrepreneurial families are often encouraged to gain diverse learning and experiences within their family, its enterprise, and beyond. They are expected to pursue such learning through all life stages. Enterprising families in South America often enroll in continuing education courses and workshops as a family. The seeds of continuous learning are often sown at a young age. For example Patricia Ghany, the Chief Financial Officer of Esau Oilfield Supplies Company Limited (ESAU) of Trinidad and Tobago, shared in her interview with *Tharawat Magazine*:

> As a young girl I worked with my mom in the accounts department and my father took me to see all the energy plants. ... I got a chance to watch him work and see how he made his contacts. After completing my MBA I worked in Europe for a few years where I taught courses in cross-cultural communication before I came back and officially joined the family company in January 1995 as CFO.

While she stresses that there was no pressure for her and her brothers to join the family business,

> it was just something that we knew we would eventually do, but we all thought that we needed to get outside work experience first.

Such learning in successful entrepreneurial families is not limited to any industry or geographic boundaries though. Robert Ettinger, the third-generation leader of a British luxury leather goods company that is named after his family, recalls his winding preparation to the top job in his family business as follows:

> I joined the family business in 1985, but everything in my life seemed to be leading up to that very moment. My parents sent me to boarding schools in Austria and France where I learnt languages and discipline. I then embarked on a business apprenticeship in a German marble stone factory, which was

also a family business, followed by experience at Mappins Fine
Jewelers in Canada. At Mappins I learnt everything about the
luxury industry by working in every division of the business.

While I was doing this, I sort of knew I was being groomed.
My father didn't force me but he saw that I had the right skills
to join the family business. I always liked doing practical things.
He had the foresight to give me the right opportunities. He was
helping me make my way towards the family business but never
by force. For a few years my passion was being a ski instructor
and I did that professionally for a while. ... My father sent me
on various business assignments and really threw me in at the
deep end.

The next generation has to want to do it and has to understand craftsmanship. If they don't it won't work. You have to
have your heart in it. You have to enjoy seeing people making
something with patience and from scratch.[32]

There is, of course, a risk in expanding the horizons of members of
the next generation—that with their enhanced experiences and skills
sets, their reliance and dependence on the family enterprise might
be reduced significantly, and they may pursue other career paths they
feel passionately about. Fully aware of this possibility, entrepreneurial
families still tend to risk it, perhaps singing these words of Khalil
Gibran: "If you love somebody, let them go, for if they return, they
were always yours. If they don't, they never were."[33] Some families,
of course, never learn to carry this tune, but successful enterprising
families do.

Money Sense *and* Emotional Sensibilities

Jane Austen's classic novel *Sense and Sensibility* is a romantic portrayal of
the life and loves of two Dashwood sisters—Elinor and Marianne. The
character of Elinor is identified with sense—good judgment and prudence—while Marianne is identified with sensibility or emotionality
—an attractive, intelligent woman who is able to love deeply. The
reader is left to decide whether sense or sensibility must triumph, often deciding on the relative importance of both and a need to balance

both approaches. Like love, money has multiple dualities and dimensions such as making and spending, earning and investing, getting and giving, losing and winning.

Money is a sensitive topic in most households and often causes disagreements among family members. Enterprising families tend to treat it as an important and complex topic of study, feeling that all its members must have basic understanding of and comfort with its multiple dimensions. Yet this learning must come from within the family, as the values and norms of each family surrounding money may vary considerably. Thus families often take active steps to imbue the basic understanding of the sense and sensibilities of money in family members

Enterprising families find ways to inculcate a desire to learn while doing something different into the mind-set of family members at a young age.

from a young age. Curt Carlson taught his daughters to conserve and invest, insisting that Marilyn take an economics course in college.[34] J. D. Power and Associates was founded by Dave and Julie Power in 1968. In its early years, often the couple and their four children would sit around the kitchen table folding J. D. Power and Associates' automobile quality questionnaires. Over time, their little company become an internationally recognized leader in customer satisfaction research and was sold to McGraw-Hill in 2005. Here is how the Power children recall their experiences around their kitchen table:

"You would try to pick the job you liked best: stuffing envelopes, putting on stamps or address labels," recalls Susan Curtin, forty-three, the youngest of the children. A common job

for younger kids was taping quarters (an incentive for people to complete the surveys) to the questionnaires, making sure the "heads" side was facing up.

The children felt very much a part of the company—and because they were paid for their work, they learned early on about the value of money. "Money could be used to get something you really want—that's a luxury—but there's also a responsibility to use it to better other people's circumstances," says Jonathan Power, forty-six, the third child.

The Power family's emphasis on working together and using money responsibly continued as the company grew. And when J.D. Power and Associates was sold in 2005, these values guided family members as they charted a new path, working together to achieve their investment and philanthropic goals.

They also commissioned a history of the company and a second book about Dave Power's fifty years in the auto industry. Retelling these stories, family members say, helped them cope with the emotional highs and lows of selling their business and clarify their priorities and goals going forward.[35]

In family life, as in business life, mastery of ambidexterity along several dimensions encourages appropriate development of entrepreneurial attitudes, thinking, and action across generations. There can be no guarantees; some family members may just not have the talents to develop or interest in the business, no matter how much they are encouraged, cajoled, threatened, or trained. On the other hand, even in families that have values, practices, and models that completely discourage transmission of entrepreneurial orientation, occasionally a truly innovative and entrepreneurial individual will somehow emerge. But enterprising families keep an eye out to develop both sides of the described ambidexterities to increase the odds a great deal.

Chapter 4

Developing Enterprising Families

Growing families and businesses are both good at consuming assets, notes John Davis,[1] a family business advisor and educator at the Harvard Business School. And the return on assets declines over time. Enterprising families continuously regenerate. When their core business is built on a unique and enduring natural setting like hot springs or on a product that endures over centuries, renewal and regeneration focuses on maintaining harmony with changes in the environment and customer needs. For example, Japanese inns like the Nishiyama Onsen Keiunkan or Houshi Ryokan (in fifty-second and forty-sixth generation of family leadership respectively) continue to evolve their services to clients, as well as management and governance of their family enterprises, even though the hot springs remain at their core. Similarly, while the Amarelli family has made licorice since 1831, harvesting and processing it in the Calabria region of southern Italy, they have embraced technological innovations and globalization to expand their product line and make their products available around the world. On the family dimension, Giuseppina Mengano Amarelli (Pina), who is married into the Amarelli family, is the face of the company. This enterprising family carefully adapts its rules for each generation to ensure it is in harmony with its context. More often, however, family enterprises move away from the original business as industries, markets, customer needs, and families evolve over time. What the enterprise did at its founding may be quite different from its focus now. For example, the Japanese Sumitomo Corporation[2] started as a company in real estate management and development in 1919, yet it is one of the largest and most diversified trading companies of Japan today.

Regardless of the form and focus of innovation, entrepreneurial efforts are necessary for the long-term survival of a family enterprise not only in older economies of Japan or Sweden but also in the emerging economies of countries like Argentina.[3] Enterprising families embrace purposeful and focused change. Yet changing amidst a backdrop of generational success and powerful personalities needs collective familial buy-in and efforts. As the family and its enterprises grow, the family needs to create structures and systems that ensure open communication

Enterprising families embrace purposeful and focused change.

and accountability while still maintaining family harmony and unity. Not only are efficient managers needed to run the current operations, equally necessary are entrepreneurial leaders who know how to make winning bets to produce the financial returns for the future.[4] And some responsible owners must provide capital for short-term needs and long-term investments. Maintaining family unity and preparing the next generation of owners, managers, and entrepreneurs require their own investments. But who is the best fit for what task must be determined. All this takes time and must be done while ensuring the everyday needs of the family and its enterprises are met.

Enterprising families are not fazed by the complexity of the task or the dedicated efforts needed to revitalize their family and business, generation after generation. They also know that leaders and entrepreneurs cannot be produced on demand or wished for but must be developed. Thus, they work hard to imbue the discipline of innovation, that

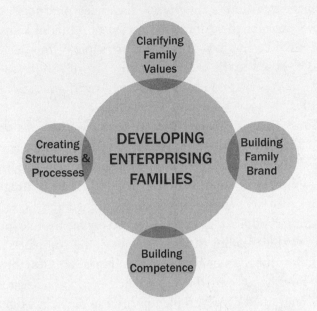

Exhibit 4.1. Four Practices to Develop Enterprising Families

is, to know systematically where and how to look for opportunities,[5] in *all* family members. Practice begins early and continues through all stages of life. Home, school, business, community, and society are treated as opportunities to learn, grow, and build capabilities. Enterprising families find four practices helpful to encourage and develop entrepreneurial leaders in the next generation.

Clarifying Family Values

"People don't buy what you do, or how you do it, but *why* you do it," argues Simon Sinek in his best-selling book *Start with Why: How Great Leaders Inspire Everyone to Take Action.*[6] *Why,* he says, is focused on core beliefs, the reason for existence, the purpose, the cause, or the essence of a leader or a company. Inspiring leaders like Martin Luther King Jr., inspirational organizations like Apple Inc., and familial teams like the Wright brothers succeed against all odds because they are built on clearly articulated simple core beliefs: "equality" for King, "challenging the status quo" for Apple, and "reliable pilot control is the key to successful flying" for Orville and Wilbur Wright. A focus on "what" directs attention to the day-to-day issues, products, or services, while "how" explains the differentiating features of a movement or an organization. This simple yet profound principle of the need to focus on *why* (as opposed to the *what* or the *how*) is well understood by enterprising families that continue to succeed over generations, against all adversities.

A business theorist analyzed thirty-centuries-old businesses and observed, "They know who they are and understand how they fit into the world."[7] These companies are an extension of the core beliefs. For example, Hallmark is built on caring, SC Johnson on integrity, Levi Strauss on creativity. The products of these legendary companies— cards, cleaning supplies, blue jeans—are merely means to express these values. Core values anchor the movements in the company. For some, like the Hall or Johnson or Strauss/Stern/Haas families, the core values or the answer to "*why* they do what they do," is already defined clearly and ingrained deeply in the upbringing of the next generation. Thus they can focus on ensuring the products/services and practices are aligned with these core values while meeting market needs. With passage of time, it is not unusual for families and companies to meander a little, and a reflective pause often helps realign priorities.

For enterprising families that have not yet examined or articulated their core values, it may be helpful to reflect on and articulate these values and how they align with the enterprise(s). In *The Secrets of Happy Families*,[8] Bruce Feiler describes how his family created its core values, the central tenets that bring self-imposed clarity of dealing with life. First, he developed a list of eighty values drawn from different sources[9] that might trigger a conversation with his wife, Linda, who was skeptical about the exercise. The couple then "aggressively" crossed out items that did not apply to them and "scribbled additions into the margins." It surprised them that since their marriage several years ago, they had not had a direct conversation about the type of family they wanted to be. Next, they engaged their twin daughters, Eden and Tybee, in the conversation. Bruce called a meeting of all four family members, asking each to come prepared with their responses to the following four items:

- Words that best describe their family
- Things most important to their family
- Family's strengths
- Sayings that best capture their family[10]

Taking turns, each shared their answers, and the discussion focused on a handful of central tenets like "we love to learn; we know that it is okay to make mistakes." The wording was tweaked over the next few days, and when all family members were comfortable with it, a written statement for the family's home was prepared. The vision of this family and the core values it wanted to uphold became clear to all, in turn guiding their conversations and decisions. In addition to articulating the core family values, such an exercise can also be useful to define the family and its boundaries, rules of entry into and exit from ownership or management, and governance roles related to the family enterprise(s).

While the Feiler family chose to "do-it-themselves" with leadership from the father, other enterprising families may prefer to engage facilitators for this exercise. Such engagement is often helpful when multiple generations are involved and the individual aspirations and expectations for the future have not been discussed. Under such circumstances, some family members of the next generation begin to feel sad or frustrated that they must suppress their aspirations to live the dreams of their seniors, and seniors may feel frustrated if they do not know what the next generation is truly interested in doing. Assumptions may be strong, and emotions may run high. Enterprising families understand that an obligatory pursuit of a career cannot lead to entrepreneurial success because excellence does not emerge from half-hearted conceptualization or constrained implementation efforts. So, they engage the best help they possibly can find for their visioning process.[11] When thinking about engaging expert help, members of enterprising families remind each other about what they might do if a member of their family took ill. Often the response is that they would do their best to get the best possible diagnosis and treatment for their family members. Just as finding the best medical expert is now a norm, enterprising families try to find the best possible help when it comes to preparing their business or family for the next level of complexity and growth.

In his classic book *Succeeding Generations*, Ivan Lansberg describes two playful activities[12] that he finds helpful to construct a "Shared Dream" for an enterprising family. In both exercises, individual aspirations of family members provide the essential raw material for the collective dream. In the first activity, individual family members

Enterprising families understand that an obligatory pursuit of a career cannot lead to entrepreneurial success because excellence does not emerge from half-hearted conceptualization or constrained implementation efforts. So, they engage the best help they possibly can find for their visioning process.

make collages using crayons, markers, magazine cutouts, drawings on iPads, and other materials *to depict the ideal life to which they aspire.* When all family members have completed their individual collages, each describes his or her creation and dream to the rest of the family. Individual renditions are then arranged into a mosaic of dreams. The common themes and patterns that emerge are then captured through symbols and words describing the shared family dream. The second activity asks each family member to write a newspaper article depicting themselves, their family, and their business five to ten years in the future. These may include accounts of future scenarios for the enterprise and roles for different family and nonfamily members. Each family member then shares his or her article with other members of the family. Together, the group then explores areas of alignment and differences. These become the raw material for envisioning the future of the family enterprise and the most appropriate roles for each member of the family.

Of course, not all parts of individuals' dreams will align with the shared familial dream. And a perfect alignment is not necessary for a family to function effectively or work towards a common purpose. With greater overlap between individual dreams, it becomes easier to carve out a shared dream and a vision for the future. At times, the visioning process clarifies that it no longer makes sense to continue the family business or for all family members to stay involved in the business. It is better to come to agreement about separation, if necessary, in this way than through an inadvertent storm of hurt feelings. By engaging trusted outsiders who don't have an actual (or perceived) conflict of interest, enterprising families try to understand the aspirations and desired futures, strengths, weaknesses, and the best-fit role within or outside the family enterprise for each key family member. This exercise is then followed by developing a career plan for each family member.

Building Family Brand

What are some of the ways that enterprising families use their family in the branding of their organization? The alignment of brand with the family name varies. A study of the websites of ninety-two of the world's oldest family companies established between 718 CE and 1761 CE found that over 75 percent of the companies highlighted their family connection to the business.[13] When the family name is concealed or downplayed, typically the organization, its products, or its location becomes the focal attention. For example, Gekkeikan, the Japanese sake maker founded in 1637, acknowledges the founder but subdues the family connection in favor of experience ("perfected brewing techniques") and a location ("well-known for its high quality of water").

With a realization of the significant impact of family firms on the community and the economy, there is a positive trend to celebrate family linkages. Astute family business leaders and advisors know the anchoring power of a clearly articulated set of core values, family story, individual aspirations, and shared dreams for the future. SC Johnson Inc., for example, proudly introduces itself as "a family company since 1886" on its website[14] and in its commercials. Through its website, the company invites[15] its customers to share their family-isms that are described as sweet, sentimental, funny, family stories of moments with loved ones. Evelyn from Neenah, Wisconsin offered the following:

> **Anne, our four-year-old granddaughter, was playing with a spring toy and was using it as a ladder for a prince. Grandpa asked, "Where did you get that ladder?" Anne said, "It was made by SC Johnson a family company." We asked her where she heard the comment—she said on TV.**

The family brand of SC Johnson is now etched in the minds of young and old alike! The core entrepreneurial values important to this family come through in how it describes its founding. The lasting effect of these stories is evident five generations later. Excerpts from the website are included below. We added italic emphasis to highlight how values supporting entrepreneurship are woven into the story of this legendary company.

> **Samuel Curtis Johnson *didn't find success quickly or easily*. But when he finally stirred it up—in a bathtub in Racine, Wisconsin—it was success that stuck. More than 120 years later, his *perseverance and commitment* remain the foundation for SC Johnson.**
>
> **Samuel Curtis Johnson set out to earn a living with the railroads. He took a job helping develop a new railway, *so confident in its potential that he invested half his salary*. And the business went bankrupt, taking his savings with it.**
>
> **Soon after, Samuel became a partner in a book and stationery store. Within a few years he had built up the capital to buy out his partner. But *despite Samuel's reputation for honesty and integrity, this business, too, failed*.**

In 1882, *nearly fifty years old, Samuel moved to Racine, Wisconsin with his family* and started over again. This time he became a parquet flooring salesman for the Racine Hardware Company. It won't surprise you to hear that after only four years, he bought out the business. ...

With just four employees, *Samuel worked diligently as salesman, bookkeeper, and business manager.* Five days a week, he toured the countryside selling flooring to contractors for fine homes, churches, hotels and public buildings. The first year, his company showed a net profit of $268.27.

Sales multiplied—and so did letters from customers who wanted help caring for their new floors. So Samuel did what any entrepreneur would do: *he rolled up his sleeves and started mixing up batches of floor wax in his bathtub.*

Samuel's *tenacity and unconventional ideas* were finally paying dividends. By the time he died in 1919, "Johnson's Wax" had become a household name in the United States and beyond.

And speaking of households ... *his son, Herbert F. Johnson, had joined the company as well.* What began in a bathtub had become a thriving family business.

But it was *always about family in the larger sense,* too. Throughout his life, Samuel *donated 10% of his income to his community—* particularly programs that supported young people. Among the many family memories of him, this *commitment to community, along with his perseverance, are the most enduring.*

It is noteworthy that the account highlights that entrepreneurial success was neither quick nor easy, as if reminding the current leaders that courage, perseverance, and commitment to the community are needed to build and grow a successful enterprise. The legacy a parent leaves to the next generation is the most significant priority for this family.

Some enterprising families use unconventional strategies to build their brand. Vipp of Denmark was started by metal worker Holger Nielsen in 1939 when he designed a rubbish bin with a pedal for his wife's hairdressing salon. As the bin gained a reputation for the functionality and design, demand for it increased in other commercial areas, such as petrol stations, ferries, hospitals, and hairdressing salons. Holger persevered in his small workshop with one employee until his death in 1992. His youngest daughter, Jette Egelund, wanted to build on the reputation for functionality and design that the bin had gained in her father's lifetime. She took over the workshop and decided to expand the market for the bins. With time, her son and daughter began working in the company. As the family did not have the funds for advertising, they thought of a creative idea—to collaborate with artists to design their bins. This innovative idea that combined utility and form helped Vipp to become an icon of the art world. Not only was the family able to attract the attention of some top artists, they were able to dramatically expand their customer base and product lines, including "the kitchen that matches the Vipp pedal bin." In 2009, the family received the highest honor in their industry when the Vipp bin was accepted in the Museum of Modern Art's permanent collection in New York. Brand building for this enterprising family has been a multigenerational effort built on the core foundation of no-nonsense practical design and genuine long-lasting materials.[16]

Enterprising families know the starting point is clarity of the core, but this is insufficient to build a family brand. Efforts to make the brand familiar are equally critical. How does your family capture the story of its enterprise? Does your company website highlight the family or its business or both equally? What message do the choices made send to your community and your customers and, most importantly, to the next generation of family members?

Building Competence

Successful enterprising families have a remarkable understanding of the need to carefully plan the career paths and learning opportunities of family members of the next generation, keeping in mind the skills needed to lead an existing enterprise and launch new ones. The practice of independent thinking and doing starts early. A family business advisor, Lee Hausner, notes that raising competent next-generation members is particularly challenging in affluent families that run successful family enterprises. When time is short, as it often is, it is easy for juniors to ask for help and for seniors to satisfy their needs. She advises against providing easy answers or access to resources. Pause, suggests Lee, count to ten. Think if some task or part of a task can be completed independently by you (or your family member). Empower yourself (or them) to come up with ideas for completing the task. Encourage such independence and celebrate it when it occurs.

Diversity of experiences helps in building confidence. An analysis of the career trajectories of 100 CEOs of the largest Italian firms[17]—58 family firms, and 42 nonfamily firms—tracked the career paths of all selected CEOs from college graduation to their first appointment as CEO. The fastest route to the CEO suite was of those individuals who accumulated and built their human capital through diverse experiences with clear accountability.

Enterprising families around the world proactively create career-development opportunities for family members of the next generation, with an eye to expanding capabilities, building confidence, and continued learning. A career plan built around both the individual's and the family's dreams can combine education, travel, working within and outside the family business in roles with clear responsibilities and accountability, and starting and growing independent ventures outside the core family business.

At Hong Kong's Automatic Manufacturing Limited (AML), a high-tech integrated manufacturing company with over 3,000 employees, Dr. John Mok, one of the founders, developed the following career and learning plan for next-generation members developed by, after discussions with the family:[18]

- Age less than 30—MSc in Technology; work as an executive in nonfamily firms;
  - Learn best practices in at least two complementary disciplines.
- Age 30–35—MSc in Marketing, coaching from corporate university and top management; work as a supervisor in the family firms;

- ○ Learn people and marketing skills.
- Age 35–40—Take an EMBA and a finance degree; co-found a start-up with AML employee (if needed) as a spin-off;
- ○ Learn startup, growth and financial management skills.
- Age 40–45—Serve industry associations; head the spin-off as general manager and serve as needed in the corporate headquarters;
- ○ Develop international strategic alliance and corporate governance experience.
- Age greater than 45—Merge the spinoff with the parent;
- ○ Learn risk management, and gain experience in mergers and acquisitions.

While this specific plan seems to work for the Mok family, others have developed their own set of career plans uniquely suited to their contexts. For example, after studying seven Latin American family enterprises, researchers Fernando Sandoval-Arzaga and Maria Fonseca-Paredes of ITESM in Mexico observed that the following mix of informal and formal actions was being used to integrate knowledge across generations and prepare the next generation of entrepreneurs.[19]

- Stage 1: From childhood to high school years:
- ○ Visit and work informally in the family business over weekends and summers.
- ○ Tell stories and narratives in informal reunions such as bedtimes and family meals.
- Stage 2: During undergraduate studies and before joining family business on a full-time basis:
- ○ Assign challenging projects with little guidance.
- ○ Go to business fairs together and share articles on family businesses.
- ○ Work outside the family business for a few years.

- Stage 3: Full-time work at the family business:

  ○ Begin with a staff position oriented toward innovation and/or strategic planning.

  ○ Build relationships with employees and other key stakeholders.

  ○ Develop a mentor-protégé relationship.

  ○ Relate family stories to the innovation process.

  ○ Create structures and process for regular formal communication among family members.

The specifics of each career plan vary significantly. But the pattern that has emerged quite clearly from studying enterprising families is that of carefully developed career plans for family members of the next generation. The most effective plans are based on thoughtful and open communications between generations, keeping an eye on the individual interests as well as the nature of challenges and opportunities in the environment. Research[20] on satisfaction and productive lifestyle after retirement reinforces the need for careful career planning not just for members of the junior generation, but for all members of an enterprising family.

Creating Structures and Processes

Education and work experiences are certainly effective ways to develop the capabilities of next-generation members. Over time, some families grow large and become complex. When an enterprise is involved, it adds complexity as the mode and degree of engagement of each family member with the enterprise varies. While some may be active majority owners, others may be passive owners; some may be leaders of the business, while others may be advisors or directors; still others may be one step removed from any of these positions but have a great influence on key decisions. Using the analogy of a stage, Australian educators and advisors Mary Barrett and Ken Moores shed light on the varied roles of women, particularly daughters, in enterprising families.[21]

Whereas the controlling owner firms are simple to govern, as all key decisions are made by one person, the sibling partnerships begin to get more complex, and cousin consortiums are the most complex of the three.[22] As the complexity increases, systems and processes need to be put into place to make decisions. Governance systems such as a family council and family offices become necessary. While the family councils become the voice of the family so all family members can be involved and engaged in the enterprise, the family office manages the financial aspects, such as investments and philanthropy. Deciding which structure is needed, setting it up, and making sure it functions as envisioned is hard work. But each provides unique learning and growth opportunities for family members.

Sylvia Shepard, a fifth-generation owner and chair of the Smith Family Council, writes that the Menasha Corporation can trace its roots to 1850 when her great-great-grandfather Elisha D. Smith moved with his new bride, Julia Mowry Smith, to Rhode Island and opened a dry goods store.[23] Over time, the company has evolved from dry goods, to butter tubs, to corrugated boxes, to reusable packaging, to point-of-purchase displays. The annual revenues crossed the $1 billion mark several years ago. With over 150 shareholders involved, the company is transitioning the leadership and ownership from the fifth to the sixth generation. In 2013, the fifth-generation family members created the Smith Family Council with an aim to improve communication among the business, board, and the family. The process of establishing the Council and its tasks are explained as follows:

> **Beginning with a family-wide survey and continuing with annual family meetings, educational panels, discussion groups, newsletters and regular surveys, the council has worked over the past nine years to give a "voice" to the family shareholders.**
>
> **With that goal largely accomplished, the council is now focused on engaging our next generation and imparting to them the entrepreneurial mind-set that each generation before them has exhibited in their approach to owning and managing the business. The council does this by encouraging them to speak out, while asking for their ideas and providing opportunities for**

them to share these ideas with senior executives. We also try to cultivate a sense of urgency about the need for them to take control.

The sixth-generation family members have said that they want to continue owning this business—or whatever this business might become. The council considers it their task to make sure that these young people understand that they are responsible for taking the company forward in a new direction—like every generation before them.[24]

Having transparent policies and accountability is clearly essential for the continuity and growth of enterprising families. However, the journey from a founder or one-person control to structures and processes that enable multiple family and nonfamily members to contribute fully and be accountable is a difficult one, fraught with high emotions and challenging discussions. With over eighty stores, today the Paris Group of Companies runs one of the largest retail chains in the Middle East. Yet when Mohammed Abdul Rahim Al Fahim, the current CEO, joined his family business on a full-time basis after graduating with a master's degree and working outside his family business for a few years, he was put in charge of the operations in Saudi Arabia. Despite his experiences in the UAE where the family was based, he felt ill-prepared to operate in this very different context. From his own experience, he learned the need to develop clear policies and systems that would allow the next-generation family members to gradually grow through the ranks of the company. Clear positions, responsibilities, ownership roles, and a board of directors had to be put into place. In an interview with *Tharawat*,[25] he observes that it is far easier to recognize the need for structure than to implement it. Emotions run high in heated family discussions when disagreements are voiced. "Being a family business doesn't necessarily mean that all members have the same principles or share the same values. There are always different perspectives," he observes. Yet as the company grows, if such systems and structures are not put in place, conflicts intensify, and it becomes difficult to maintain accountability or prepare the next generation for leadership roles. The journey was long and arduous as it required sacrifices that some family members were not prepared to make. He wanted to get the new structures and policies developed and implemented in eighteen months, but it took him almost four years. And even now, he finds the policies must be updated every quarter as new issues come up. Yet after having gone through the process, he feels that while he wants his children to join the business, they now have means to help each member of the next generation to mature by giving them responsibilities they can shoulder and enabling their development over time.

Being a family business doesn't necessarily mean that all members have the same principles or share the same values.

It is time consuming to understand and implement the structures and processes needed for longevity and growth. Some enterprising families use economic downturns to focus on such issues. ABC Recycling has been in the scrap business since 1912, when Joseph Yochlowitz and his wife, Sarah, moved from Poland to Canada. When the fourth-generation family member David joined the company on a full-time basis in 1988, they employed thirty-five people. As the operations had expanded, the family desired to develop a strong team of professional family and nonfamily managers. For example, one policy in the shareholders agreement from a previous generation prohibited spouses of family members from working at ABC. To learn from other enterprising families and experts on how to transition to such professionalization and develop company policies that would reflect the changed contexts, they became active participants in the Canadian Association of Family Enterprises (CAFE). This national not-for-profit association has a mandate to promote the well-being and success of families in business. With the help of a consultant, the family talked about such sensitive issues and developed new policies that were unanimously accepted. As this family has a long tradition of giving to the community, it created a new position—manager of community relations—to oversee the philanthropic and community activities of the family. Paid for by the family enterprise, this position had clear accountability including oversight of the career development for family members of the next generation. Fourth-generation family member Karen Bichin, who was previously in charge of the human resource department, was named to this position. In an interview with *Family Business Magazine,* she noted, "2012 was a challenging year in our industry, but now things are picking up. We used that slow time to identify areas that needed improvement, and we've come out stronger. We're feeling good about the business, the family and the foundation we've set for moving forward in our next 100 years."[26]

Once structures and systems are in place, opportunities for next-generation engagement increase. For example, some families develop junior boards. The job of the chair of the meeting is rotated. The leader is expected to develop an agenda, decide who may and may not talk and when, write the minutes and make sure they are circulated in a timely manner, and follow up if action items fall in their domain as well. Small yet meaningful tasks with a clear outcome are assigned to this board. One family asked the junior board to determine the policy for usage of a family vacation home. Another asked their next-generation board to plan and design the family retreat.

Enterprising families that embrace lifelong learning continue to educate themselves in the leading-edge thinking on how to develop and use these structures. For example, Nan-b and Philippe de Gaspe Beaubien, founders of a major Canadian telecommunications company and the Business Families Foundation, continue to learn about how to prepare their family and its members for entrepreneurial success. They regularly participate in family business workshops and educational programs. Every time they travel to a new city around the world, they make it a point to visit other enterprising families who have been running successful businesses over generations so they can learn from their experiences and stories.[27]

In closing, enterprising families know they can choose from a large and growing arsenal of ideas to ensure each interested family member is well prepared for a productive and satisfactory career, either within the current family enterprise or with a new one that generates future revenues. Perhaps the simplest way to stay in touch with the leading-edge thinking and practices of enterprising families is to become regular readers of family business specific magazines and to attend each year at least one conference or educational program focused on family businesses. Such programs are often designed to help multiple family members learn together. Families that learn together, grow together!

WORK SHEET 4

4A: Our Family's Values and Brand

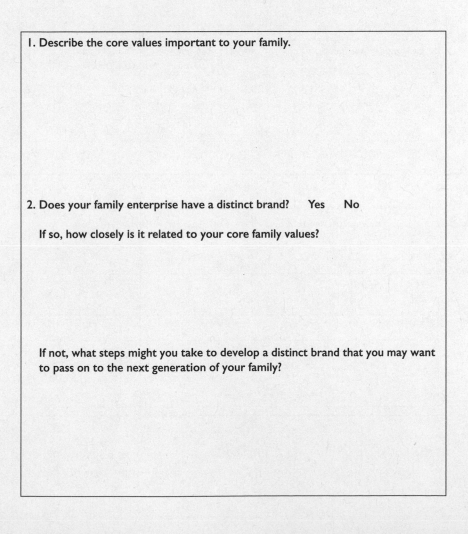

1. Describe the core values important to your family.

2. Does your family enterprise have a distinct brand?   Yes   No

   If so, how closely is it related to your core family values?

   If not, what steps might you take to develop a distinct brand that you may want to pass on to the next generation of your family?

4B: Career Plan Focused on Competence Building

1. What are the most important capabilities needed for your family enterprise to succeed?

2. Develop a career plan for yourself, and then discuss it with another family member of a different generation.

NAME _____

Age Range	Education	Work Experience	Capabilities to Learn

If the family might benefit from such an activity, engage several others in discussing how to create similar development plans for all family members.

Chapter 5

SECRETS OF ENTREPRENEURIAL ORGANIZATIONS

It is always challenging to create organizations whose structures and practices produce the kind of people and behavior that help them grow and renew. Building a family business that can last past the founding generation by utilizing practices that sustain entrepreneurial thinking and action has its own extra challenges—and some potential advantages.

Family businesses that remain private, for example, are able to think and act more for the long term than just the short term. Because they are not driven by the requirement to predict, report, and precisely deliver quarterly earnings, they can dedicate the inherently lengthy time needed to challenge, nurture, and develop their people.[1] A powerful vision for the business, along with the long tenures of family business leaders[2] to reinforce it, can also help create a culture that fosters growth and innovation.

In this chapter we will discuss what is known about design conditions that encourage entrepreneurial initiative from all areas and levels of the organization, thereby raising the odds of generating new products, processes, practices, and structures—and even new businesses. Then we will apply the knowledge to family firms. Organizations best accomplish their goals when their design fits with their strategic objectives.[3] Organizational structure and mechanisms are like paved pathways that encourage people to walk along them, guiding desired behavior that will accomplish organizational—and where built in—family objectives. Without organizational design, coordinated behavior would be accidental and random.

As with many good intentions, however, not all sensible ones are followed. Sometimes signals are misread. Sometimes pathways are so well traveled they become ruts. Sometimes as conditions change, new pathways or routines are called for, but habits die hard.[4] It can even be necessary to do some painful pruning of recalcitrant family members or long-serving nonfamily members who no longer fit current conditions.[5] The idea is to make the odds as favorable as possible to encourage as much initiative, as much innovation, and as much entrepreneurial behavior as possible throughout the family company.

In what follows we are using the terms *innovation* and *entrepreneurial behavior* interchangeably. The conditions that stimulate greater innovation are mostly the same ones that will stimulate more entrepreneurial behavior throughout the organization. Both are about constantly seeking improved ways of doing things, although it takes the implementation of entrepreneurship to make innovations come to fruition. Family enterprises are particularly strong when it comes to implementing new ideas, even though they often take longer to decide what innovations to undertake.[6] It isn't necessary to have every organizational mechanism aligned for innovation, but it is likely that at least several are needed. Enterprising families take their time; they tend to stagger innovations, both in terms of the degree of changes and the parts or processes of organizations or of families in which change is undertaken.[7] However, they can move rapidly when they have to. Even relatively traditional older businesses, like the Japanese Houshi Inn and the Italian Amarelli Liqourice companies that you learned about in the previous chapter, which use deep product knowledge and gradual incremental innovations to adapt to customer interests, can change as needed. Of course, none of these elements guarantee permanence. Kongo Gumi, a Japanese company that lasted as a family business for 1,400 years, had to be sold in 2006. Specializing in Buddhist temple construction, the company took on too much debt during the 1980s bubble in Japan, after which contributions to temples declined, slowing construction.[8]

Not all family companies, however, have the advantage of being in a unique location or having a specialty product, nor have they created organizations that develop entrepreneurial attitudes and behavior in all generations. Too many family companies operate under conditions that make needed innovation difficult or discourage new ideas, so they are only a byproduct of random bursts of talent in the family. At their worst, these kinds of companies can lack many growth conditions and are genuinely stultifying.

Enterprising families ... tend to stagger innovations, both in terms of the degree of changes and the parts or processes of organizations or of families in which change is undertaken.

Imagine working in a family business where your role was determined early on the basis of your gender or birth order, or of a senior family member's hunch about what you would be good at, or by a strong need that existed when you started. Then imagine being stuck in that role or function for most of your career. Imagine also that the organization had many fixed ways of doing things that everyone was expected to follow, a very clear but restricted concept of just what business it was in, strong top-down directions and control, prescribed communication patterns, rigid organizational silos with little interaction across them, constrained and tightly controlled resources available only once a year or only through one executive, and a general culture that discouraged straying far from what is known and predictable.

Few family businesses would share all of these characteristics, yet many family members have been faced with organizations that are similarly constrained. Although there is some reason to believe that the conventional wisdom about how few family businesses survive into the third generation or to the fourth is exaggerated,[9] there is ample evidence that without adaptation, expiration is imminent.[10] In non-supportive environments there are occasional exceptions, with some individual entrepreneurial family members bursting through the inhibitions that only reinforce the status quo. Extraordinarily gifted individuals, rebellious people who can't keep themselves from testing all authority, or a sudden death or serious illness that thrusts the younger individual into an unexpected senior role all can yield surprise stars. Still, the odds are low that a younger generation of family members will learn to be entrepreneurial or acquire the characteristics needed to invigorate and renew a business if enterprises have few supportive mechanisms or structures for such learning. And in turn, nonfamily members, increasingly also needed for their ideas and contributions, won't learn either. It is very hard to overcome an array of organizational forces blocking entrepreneurial initiative. Yet enterprising families don't wait for such rebellion or for the most capable members of the next generation to exit from the family business system. Rather they make sure the system is attractive so the most capable next-generation members will want to spend their energy and career to grow and develop the enterprise.

Building organizations to generate innovative, entrepreneurial behavior requires balancing numerous elements, a skill we call ambidexterity. Careful hands on control, paying attention to detail to preserve ongoing operations—operational excellence—is an important part of successful longevity. But in a rapidly changing world, it is increasingly important to find ways to develop new products, services, and processes. Therefore, because innovation is an important challenge for organizations of all kinds, considerable attention has been paid to how to generate it. Let us start with a high-level overview about what has been discovered, in general, about the many different organizational conditions that encourage innovative behavior and increase the odds that innovative behavior will occur throughout the organization, family business or not. We then add the potential challenges or minefields for family businesses, which alert us to why some of the practices are so difficult to implement, although some aspects of family businesses actually support innovation. Then we look at intriguing examples of how some family companies are using these conditions well and what else can be concluded about what organizations might do.

Organizational Conditions Encouraging Innovation and Entrepreneurial Behavior

Broadly speaking, the organizational conditions that encourage entrepreneurial behavior can be categorized as *supportive leadership, high levels of employee empowerment, an experimental culture,* and *risk management.*[11] *Supportive leadership* means that there are expectations of high and improving performance but no penalties for well-intended, thoughtful failures. In addition, the voice of the customer, present and potential, is "brought inside" the organization, and there is constant focus on their views.

Employee empowerment includes reduced hierarchy and flatter organizations that reduce segmentation or boundaries between units; small units with many cross-functional teams that have learned to think holistically and take reasonable, bounded risk; broad assignments and education that encourage initiative and experimentation, assignments for learning and gradually increased decision-making, risk-taking, job variety, and autonomy as well as performance; and open access to information. In addition, there are ample rewards and recognition; investment-oriented rewards not just based on past performance; modern HR practices and procedures; on-boarding, acculturation, and training; honest, developmental performance evaluation; and flexible working hours.

An *experimental culture* includes a learning environment that encourages action and experimentation, trial and error, explicit problem solving and discovery, observation of and feedback from peers as well as superiors, self-reflection, and introspection.

Risk management entails multiple organizational side bets so that units that require detailed operational excellence receive needed attention and control, while new, unproven opportunities can operate much more fluidly. Also, there may need to be discretionary venture funds outside of regular operating budgets.

Careful hands on control, paying attention

to detail to preserve ongoing operations—

operational excellence—is an important part of

successful longevity. But in a rapidly changing

world, it is increasingly important to find ways to

develop new products, services, and processes.

Not every single condition need be present to encourage entrepreneurial behavior; taken together they serve as signals indicating the organization's desired direction and behaviors. No company gets it right all the time, and very few are skilled at all of these, but there are positive examples of each to learn from.

(Note that all of these points about organizational conditions are for generating innovations or entrepreneurial behavior, and they work best at the stage of idea generation. To get ideas flowing, a more participative leadership style works best. But as illuminated by the concept of ambidexterity, which embraces differing organization methods for different phases, more directive, assertive leadership behaviors work better for moving innovations toward implementation.[12])

Barriers and reinforcers for innovation and entrepreneurship in family businesses. Some of the natural features of family business can get in the way of innovation and entrepreneurship. For example, past successes of the company can create an attachment to the way things have been done and a desire not to rock the golden boat. Executives may have long tenure so that there is a set way of doing things and resistance to change out of habit or lack of knowledge of alternatives. The family investments and fortune may be completely tied into one firm, reducing the propensity to take risks out of natural desire to protect wealth. If financial decisions are restricted only to family members, there may be limited expertise for assessing the likelihood of success of unfamiliar innovation possibilities.

On the other hand, family businesses have some natural advantages that are often overlooked. Relatively low formalization, lesser resource dependence on external capital providers, and relatively greater willingness to follow the lead from the top all support possible quick action.[13] The longer tenure of senior executives can also mean longer-term thinking about investments and their payoff. As noted previously, families may be slower to take innovative decisions, but once they are made they usually can implement more rapidly than other companies.

Ambidexterity: The Need for Both Innovation and Operational Excellence[14]

We have observed numerous dimensions of ambidexterity mastered in progressive entrepreneurial family firms that could generate innovation generation after generation. This form of nimbleness, of being able to utilize opposite qualities when appropriate, helps nurture innovation, develop entrepreneurial behavior among family (and non-family) members of the next generation, and preserve the firms over time. The dimensions we will discuss are:

- Incremental, progressive, *and* radical innovations
- Balancing focus on the past, present *and* future
- High standards *and* allowance for failure
- Balancing widespread input about decisions *with* rapid decision-making
- Family control *and* professionalization
- Strong family bonds *and* wide bridges to external communities

Incremental, progressive, *and* radical innovations. Three different kinds of innovation can result from entrepreneurial leadership, structures and practices, with each kind valuable at times. And since over time all three forms of innovation ought to be going on with some kind of exploration, the work can be divided based on interests, capability, and energy of family members of different generations, as well as nonfamily members of different generations. This aids in keeping the entrepreneurial spirit circulating throughout the enterprise and the enterprising family.

> *All these firms create a culture of innovation, where it is expected that innovation is a natural part of what the firm does, not an intruder threatening a good thing.*

The most dramatic form, and the one many people think of when talking about innovation, though least common, is *radical* or *break-through* innovation,[15] where an entirely new industry, product category, or way of doing business is created and sustained. This is the most profound and far-reaching type when successful. Although certainly desirable and extremely profitable when successful, it is relatively rare, and the odds are against it. Great investments, time, and ability to take risks are needed. For example, the French family company Michelin, founded in 1888, grew to be the largest tire company in the world (currently the second-largest) by inventing the steel-belted radial tire and dedicating years and years of development and investment to actually be able to produce them. They did this in the face of great derision from other tire manufacturers, along with plenty of internal opposition. At the same time, once the basic design was perfected, there was obsessive attention to driving down the cost curve and increasing reliability, as well as designing innovative and mobile equipment to expand manufacturing to other parts of the world.[16]

At the other end of the spectrum is *incremental* or *constant innovation*, in which people at every level are making frequent minor adjustments to everyday problems while doing their jobs. These kinds of innovations most engage people at every level and help keep profits coming in while they are working on and waiting for breakthroughs. Although family-controlled Toyota, for example, is also a breakthrough leader in hybrid cars, for years it also produced reliable cars, quietly utilizing a system that produces tens of thousands of useful small changes year after year, initiated by people at all levels of the organization, starting with the shop floor.[17] Many organizations would be delighted to achieve this kind of innovation; individually most are minor but in aggregate potentially very impactful.

The third kind of innovations might be called *progressive*, and they are made by applying a known tool or technique to adjacent territories. This might lead to new products, extensions of existing business lines, new applications of an existing technology to a different area, and so on. These can be highly profitable innovations. Jean Roze, a French producer of high-quality silk upholstery since 1650, has maintained its very high-quality silk production while extending its business to other materials:

> Today, the company, under the management of Antoinette Roze, daughter of Jean Roze, a member of the twelfth generation, continues to develop its specialization in the weaving of silk upholstery fabrics for a professional clientele in France and abroad. ... [I]t is able to implement its very extensive know-how, gained on silk, to other materials such as cotton, viscose, wool or linen, in order to obtain a variety of fabrics, a characteristic development of a family company which has been able to see its future, from generation to generation, without even for a moment lowering its requirements or losing its profound respect for quality.[18]

Another Japanese family company, Toraya, founded in 1526, makes special high-quality confections.[19] They consider themselves dedicated to innovation, but it has been of the incremental variety for centuries.

The core product remains the same, but quality is constantly improved, new equipment has been developed, and a few non-company shops in Japan were allowed to carry the line. With Western-style confections becoming more popular in Japan, and the long-term demand for their product declining, major innovations are being considered—opening up in countries other than France (Paris) and adding a US distributor —which is challenging because it calls for new skills and people, in addition to quality refinements.

All these firms create a culture of innovation, where it is expected that innovation is a natural part of what the firm does, not an intruder threatening a good thing. Policies and practices, as later described, encourage ideas and initiative throughout the organization. The next graphic provides a visual representation of how the various forms of innovation can be part of the design of the family organization, each serving different functions.

We want to sound a cautionary note, however. Although from time to time enterprising families may have to focus more on one

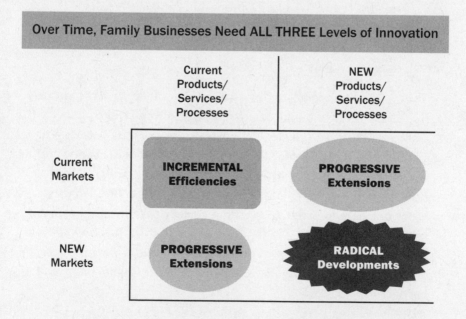

Figure 5.1. Three Innovation Levels in Family Enterprises

form of innovation in their organizations, they are well aware that it is *ambidexterity* along the innovation dimensions that leads to long-term success. They must balance the ability to innovate with the ability to preserve and sustain existing valuable activities and must exercise good judgment about when to emphasize the new over the old and in what proportion. Family members across the generations do not have to be the ones who think of every possible innovation. But they need to perpetuate the organization that stimulates innovative ideas and experiments, tests them, chooses the best ones, and supports their implementation, all the while protecting the existing core business(es). The founders' individual genius is often exaggerated in hindsight; different generations and family members can play different valuable roles in keeping entrepreneurship and core activities alive. Without that, the family business will either stagnate or kill the goose laying the golden eggs while pursuing new activities. Though it is important to generate entrepreneurial activity, it is also important to know how to contain it in order to keep extracting value from more traditional activities.[20]

As a dramatic example, take the experience of Lego, a well-known family company founded in Denmark in 1932 by Ole Kirk Kristiansen. In the 1990s, after years of rapid growth, the company thought it could leverage its brand and leap into several new areas, including watches, clothing, and entertainment. In a few years, sales had fallen and debt piled up. It had to retrench to the basic toy-building-block business to restore growth.

> **"We were getting off track and realized that having a strong brand wasn't enough," said Jørn Lykke Strange, vice president Nordic/Benelux at Lego, remembering those troubled times. The valuable lesson learned was that "[e]ven if you are good at developing and offering play sets based on construction toys, that doesn't necessarily make you the best movie producer. We learnt that through the difficult years."**
>
> **At some point the tradition of innovation that had been a cornerstone of Lego since it was founded, converted into an obsession for launching new products in areas in which it had no experience. The company believed that the brand and the**

name reputation built through decades would be enough. It was wrong—and probably no one was telling them."[21]

With innovation, judgment and balance are needed. Determining how much to support the past is as important as not being trapped by it.

Balancing focus on the past, present, *and* future. A related form of managing contradictions, as suggested by the Lego example, is knowing how to balance proper attention and honor to the past with awareness of current issues involving changing consumer demands, new competitors, technology shifts, alterations in supply, and anything else that can render previously successful practices less effective—all while being able to think long term to address problems and opportunities of the future.

Corning Glass Works, founded in New York in 1851 by Amory Houghton in the glass industry, has been particularly strong at perpetual investment in research and development, always looking for new products that can serve growing markets. It has such a great commitment to addressing the future that it has sold or closed some traditional successful businesses in order to have sufficient funds to invest in high-opportunity products still building on their glass expertise, such as fiber optics. Yet, like Michelin, once it creates a product, the company gives enormous attention to using constant process improvement to drive down costs and ward off competition.[22] And like Michelin, Corning made very long-term bets on products that others weren't even considering, as it looked out at how needs would change with emerging technologies. Yet both companies also made continuous incremental innovation part of how they came to see vast new opportunities. For example, Corning evolved from light bulbs to radio tubes to TV picture tubes, and then to glass fiber, always trying to anticipate new applications by combining constant improvement with breakthrough thinking. They have been good at past, present, and future focus.

High standards *and* allowance for failure. A closely related pair of seeming opposites is the devotion to very high standards of performance along with a tolerance for experimentation and failure. It is seldom easy for top managers to tolerate mistakes, especially when they have made numerous good choices (and perhaps forgotten the times when they went down wrong paths and had to shift course). Yet to create widespread innovative and entrepreneurial behavior, experimentation and learning must happen.[23] Occasionally the opposite is true, and senior managers are too forgiving of sloppy performance because they fear not being liked.

One stellar example is the WL Gore Company, founded in 1958 by Wilbert Lee Gore and his wife, Vieve Gore. This innovative family company has clothing, electronics, medical, and industrial divisions. Because of its commitment to innovation, it has developed over 1,000 products in these diverse industries. Learning and exploration are built into the company, with all employees having considerable autonomy, and 10 percent of their time as "dabble time" to explore anything they think might eventually become a viable product. Anyone with an idea can try to recruit other employees to give some of their time to help. If they can find willing help that is one sign that they are probably onto something interesting, but if not, it indicates that they may be heading down a dead end. The initial test of the idea, therefore, happens early on as peers decide whether or not to join in. Furthermore, there are frequent peer reviews of performance and high expectations that everyone will be contributing and stretching. The low levels of bureaucracy and considerable autonomy make the company one of the "best places to work."[24]

Companies organized to promote innovation often have dramatic stories about top leaders praising good experiments that didn't work, along with plenty of smaller experiments and failures, then learning from the results. The challenge is to keep the failures to a manageable level, to resist finger-pointing and "I told you so's," and to keep learning.

Balancing widespread input about decisions *with* rapid decision-making. Innovative companies get much better results when all parts of the organization have a voice and when new ideas come from outside. Yet at times continued discussion would delay important decisions and cause missed opportunities. This is especially true when being a first or early mover would provide an extensive advantage. Although certain features of family businesses, such as emotional ties to existing assets and rigid mental models of what creates success, often lead to resistance to radical innovation, these can be overcome with practices that reduce barriers to communication and information.

Not only does the family connection allow for long-term investment, but if family members can find ways to open up their sources of knowledge and models of how things work, they benefit even further. This is especially effective for adoption of discontinuous technologies, where flexibility and trial and error are needed. For example, the family-owned Otto Group of Germany became the second-largest

It is seldom easy for top managers to tolerate mistakes, especially when they have made numerous good choices (and perhaps forgotten the times when they went down wrong paths and had to shift course). Yet to create widespread innovative and entrepreneurial behavior, experimentation and learning must happen.

online retailer in the world by deliberately developing complementary knowledge in e-commerce and using their patient capital to make cautious but continuing investments in Internet retailing to overcome numerous failures to move online. It is difficult but vital to expose family executives to outside ideas and allow for constructive conflict about tasks and processes.[25]

For another example of being open to outside influences but still being able to make rapid decisions when necessary, consider Tetra Pak AB. Established in Sweden in 1951 by Ruben Rausing with help from his wife, this company leads the world in liquid food processing and packaging. Although the company partners closely with many different customers and has company engineers working with them on every aspect of their businesses, it can make major decisions with just one or two phone calls and a quick discussion with the senior managers.

In some other companies family members do not get involved at all in day-to-day operations. They may even be prohibited from taking operating roles but use board roles to stay attentive enough to understand what is going on and to make investment decisions quickly. Globally, an increasing number of companies have some nonfamily senior executives but still maintain family control at the board level.[26]

Family control *and* professionalization. Related to maintaining central, rapid family decision-making is the need to balance family control with increased professionalization of the organization and senior management as the world becomes more complex. That requires more formal techniques for analytical decision-making.

A group of successful, multigenerational, innovative German family companies share a common approach to balancing professionalization and use of nonfamily members with family control. Routine, incremental, operational innovation is expected of the ongoing organization, but more radical innovation is held to be the province of founders and family members. One reason for this caution is the longer time horizon required for more radical moves. They have all made it work for them.[27]

One of the largest and most successful family firms to sustain both family engagement and professionalization is Walmart. The family still retains control of the company despite large public holdings of shares, but it utilizes professional managers extensively. Yet it isn't necessary for family firms to become gigantic to move towards professionalization along with family control. Pharma Co and Construct Co are two Spanish (Catalan) companies [names disguised] working on keeping family control while also increasing professionalism by bringing in nonfamily members into managerial positions. Especially in Construct Co, the senior generation is not highly educated and has always made decisions intuitively, while at 170-plus-year-old Pharma Co, which also started with an intuitive founder, the process of professionalization has gone through several stages, going as far as selecting an outside CEO.[28] And we would be remiss if we did not point out that family or nonfamily members can be professional (or unprofessional), following (or not) the best practices of what business professionals do. As even a cursory reading of the business press would make clear and research bears out, not all independent managers behave independently or without bias, nor are all family member managers unable to act objectively and professionally.[29]

Development of leadership abilities of both family members *and* nonfamily members. Increasingly, as companies grow and the world becomes more complex, they find it necessary to invest in the development of employees at all levels. That helps support some of the other ambidexterities already mentioned. Here is a strong example of working to develop both family and nonfamily members to keep the business innovative.

In 1845, Samuel Curtis founded Curtis Packaging in Connecticut to manufacture fancy combs and buttons. These required protective, rigid boxes for shipping, which turned out to be more efficiently produced on-site. Through four generations of family, the company evolved into a leading producer of innovative custom packaging. The company was then sold to five executives, who within ten years wanted to retire. They sold it to Don Droppo Sr., who was a partner at the company's accounting firm. After discouraging his son from joining the company in case it turned out not to be viable, Don Sr. realized that his son could bring needed talent and invited him to join in the early 2000s. Curtis Packaging once again became a family company, but this time run by the Droppo family instead of the founding Curtis family. Soon after, Don Sr. brought in a senior executive to run operations while Don Jr. learned more about the business. By 2010 Don Jr. became president and CEO, and his father became chairman of the board. With this leadership team, Curtis Packaging became the industry leader for environmentally responsible packaging.[30]

Innovative family firms design the organization both around systems and individuals. They value, develop, and celebrate the rare and extraordinary individuals who have entrepreneurial and innovative intuition, but they don't shut out everyone else. Increasingly, effectiveness requires collaboration and teamwork, bringing together people with different specialties and knowledge to create successful innovation. Yet they try to preserve space and recognition for the unusually talented and creative stars, family members and others, when they appear. Nonfamily firms can find this harder to do because out of beliefs in fairness and order, they are more likely to insist that everyone follow predetermined roles and rules.

Innovative family firms design the organization both around systems and individuals.

For example, today an enormous infrastructure firm in South India, KPRT (disguised name) started its life as a bank in 1993. Although the firm's strong founder made decisions by command and built the firm, KPRT has been able to develop shared leadership in the next generation. This was done by creating formal mechanisms and governance rules for operating the business, family council, and business board and by developing shared vision, strategy, and values to induce moderate cohesion and capacity for conflict resolution. All three next-generation members are very capable, and with their father's guidance they have agreed to take positions in the business that fit their respective strengths. Yet they will rotate periodically to expand knowledge and preserve equal status. That way they exercise collective decision making, yet also allow individual domains by expertise.[31]

We should acknowledge that it might be possible for some companies with talented family members to innovate successfully without investing in the development of nonfamily members. This is possible in modest-sized firms in industries like finance where expertise at the

top can be relatively more important than depth of managerial expertise. Over time, this is likely to lead to the diminishing of innovation and entrepreneurial behavior because luck doesn't always produce
shooting stars in the family firmament on schedule.

**Family closeness reinforced *along with* widespread external contacts
and networks.** Another perhaps paradoxical combination is the reinforcing of family cohesion even while venturing further into industry
associations and other external groups, where new contacts are made,
techniques are learned, business opportunities are discovered, and
even changing social attitudes have a chance for exposure and change.
For example, at Pharma Co mentioned before, a profound shift was
created by attendance at International Forum on Enterprise (IEF),
Family Business Network (FBN), and the Family Firm Institute, as
noted by Jorge, the youngest brother of the fifth generation:

> **We saw that in the twenty-first century, it made no sense hav-
> ing my sister out of the family business. This old tradition was
> no longer valid or defensible. Therefore, we decided to incor-
> porate her as a shareholder. We discussed this idea with my
> father who supported us. He too sensed that this was the right
> direction, as he also saw from his friends that this was the gen-
> eral drift of things.**[32]

Another variation of family closeness combined with many external
contacts was part of McCain Foods, one of the largest manufacturers
of French fries and potato specialties, which started in a small town in
New Brunswick, Canada. The founding brothers were extremely close,
hard workers who traveled everywhere together, making the company
visible and forming many partnerships around the world. They were
inseparable for a long time, using a common vision of rapid growth and
an emphasis on innovation in operations to reinforce the family while
making profitable partnerships. Unfortunately, almost forty years later
they ended up in a feud over choosing a family successor, though company success continued.[33] Outside contacts do not necessarily break up
the family, nor does family closeness guarantee closeness forever.

At Tetra Pak, multiple customer relationships were developed and built into partnerships, even though that helped with keeping tight family control. While new ways may be learned and migrated into the family, external exposure is necessary to keep innovation going without harming family cohesion.

Conclusions. In addition to an overview of what is known about creating innovative organizations, we have focused on critical areas where ambidexterity is valuable for managing the innovation in family businesses. We have tried to give a variety of examples of what families are doing in each of these dimensions to get a sense of the range of possibilities.

Designing the organization to foster skill at ambidexterity—balancing risk-taking innovation with excellent execution of existing businesses—is necessary for building entrepreneurial leadership in the next generation. Not every element that encourages innovation is required (though all reinforce each other), but conservative, risk-avoidant firms will need shifts in terms of welcoming new ideas, an experimental attitude, willingness to allow next-generation and junior people opportunities to learn, and the capacity for knowing how to allow experimentation while also preserving the best of existing practices. Without at least some movement in this direction, dire consequences in the family business may increase: business decay, talented next-generation members leaving (or never entering) the business, and bitter family feuds, lawsuits, or other signs of major frustration. It is also worth mentioning that brilliant innovative ideas might be coming from a member of the founding generation that seem too extreme to be explored—wisely or foolishly—with equally dire results.

In the next chapter, we will go deeper into how to create the kind of organization that greatly increases the odds of producing future generations of entrepreneurial leadership. We examine how a number of companies are actually able to implement these important yet very challenging conditions. As tough as it is, you can make headway no matter what position you are currently occupying.

WORK SHEET 5

Inventory of Organizational Conditions Supporting
Entrepreneurial/Innovative Behavior

Complete as much of the following as you can, and then discuss with members of your family currently active in your business. You will benefit most if you discuss this with at least one family member who is from the other generation (junior if you are the senior, or vice versa).

---

1. In the last five years, can you provide examples of different levels of innovation by your company?

DEGREE OF INNOVATION*	FOCUS OF INNOVATION				
	Products/ Services	Markets/ Customer Segments	Processes	Governance System	Family Systems
Incremental					
Progressive					
Breakthrough/ Radical					

*Degrees of Innovation

Incremental innovation is one where people at every level are making frequent minor adjustments to everyday problems while doing their jobs.

Progressive innovation is the application of a known tool or technique to adjacent territories. This might lead to new products, extensions of existing business lines, new applications of an existing technology to a different area, and so on.

Breakthrough or radical innovations are those where an entirely new industry, product category, or way of doing business is created and sustained.

2. A quick diagnosis of the current level of entrepreneurial preparedness of your family enterprise:

How important is each of the following for the longevity of your family enterprise?	1 Not at all important	2	3 Moderately important	4	5 Critical
Clear entrepreneurial vision reinforced constantly, everyone is expected to contribute to innovation at all levels as part of their jobs					
Constant expectations of high, improving performance, with no penalties for failures (unless repeated)					
High levels of empowerment					
Many experiments, small units with cross-functional teams, learning to think holistically, taking reasonable, bounded risks					
Reduced hierarchy, flatter organizations, and reduced segmentation or boundaries between units					
Open access to information, ample rewards and recognition (stock or its equivalent)					
Broad assignments and education, encouragement of initiative and experimentation, assignments for learning, gradual decision-making, risk-taking					
A learning culture that encourages action and experimentation, trial and error, explicit problem solving and discovery, observation of and feedback from peers as well as superiors, self-reflection and introspection					
Onboarding, acculturation of newcomers					

Voice of the customer "brought inside"					
Investment-, not just performance-oriented rewards					
Discretionary dedicated venture funds outside of regular operating budgets					
Multiple organizational side bets so that units that require detailed operational excellence can receive the type of attention and control needed, while new, unproven opportunities can operate much more fluidly					
Professionalization of the board					
Family members wanting to work in the business or within it are expected to prove themselves					
Culture of hands-on support from leadership					

3. Action Planning. Select the items you listed 4 or 5 in the previous table. For each, indicate the current performance of your family enterprise as follows:

Not good at all (*)   Moderate (**)   Excellent (***)

List the items you would like to work on this year as a pilot. How might you go about making them happen? How would you prepare your family and organization for related changes? How will you measure the success (or failure) of each initiative?

Items to work on within next two years	Steps to make them happen	Success or Failure measures to be used

Chapter 6

DEVELOPING ENTREPRENEURIAL
ORGANIZATIONS

Redesigning a successful enterprise to accomplish new strategic objectives is hard. A recent McKinsey study found that 60 percent of a large group of global executives had tried organizational redesigns within the past two years but less than 25 percent of their efforts had succeeded.[1] Enterprising families with a long-term orientation, determined to foster all levels of innovation—incremental, progressive, and breakthrough—while maintaining the core business find ways to accomplish this challenging task. It takes more than selecting some of the organizational characteristics that promote innovation and announcing them. Effective redesign and implementation requires careful planning linked to the long-term innovation objectives, understanding the current state of the organization to be sure that changes take current conditions into account, recognizing that not just roles and reporting relationships have to change but also actual practices and policies, seeing that the right people—family as well as nonfamily members—are put in place, and working hard at communicating clearly at all levels and managing the transition and its attendant risks while moving from the current state of the organization to the desired new one.[2]

The good news is that fostering entrepreneurial innovations of all kinds does not have to depend on unusual geniuses with extraordinary foresight, unlimited funds, indefinite time, and no competition.

Although very few breakthrough innovations have had some of those elements, most of the incremental and progressive innovations that fuel organizational improvements over time do not work that way. It isn't that the usual analytic tools—and their strengths, weaknesses, opportunities, and threats—don't come into the picture, especially in predictive situations where the likely outcomes are known, risks are low, and only incremental innovation are desired. Instead, analysis doesn't have to be comprehensive and all-encompassing where a new unknown possibility is being considered and can't really be predicted in advance. Through a cycle of acting quickly, learning, reshaping current activities into new action, relearning, and deciding in advance what losses are the limit, the enterprising family can tackle the unknown. An example from Colombia at the end of this chapter shows this process in action. But how was it discovered?

In the late 1990s Saras Sarasvathy, a researcher from Carnegie Mellon University,[3] traveled across seventeen US states to meet with thirty founders of companies that ranged in value from $200 million to $6.5 billion and spanned a variety of industries such as steel, railroads, teddy bears, semiconductors, and bio-technology. The aim was to understand how these serial entrepreneurs repeatedly transformed their ideas into enduring firms that grew so rapidly.[4] They were asked to solve entrepreneurial problems while talking out loud rather than describing retrospectively how they had become successful. Patterns emerged despite the many different backgrounds of these entrepreneurs. These patterns have been further developed by researchers at Babson College[5] and the Kellogg School of Management.[6] Entrepreneurs look at their skills and what they know, along with the resources at their disposal and who might help them, so they can find and quickly test ideas to discover whether they can lead to something useful and valuable. The entrepreneurs start some kind of action so they can find out quickly and inexpensively whether the idea might be a real possibility or whether it needs modification. They then decide how they can do the next experiment, pilot project, or test run to learn more, in an iterative cycle. This eventually leads to a new product, business, or process or to a decision to give that up and move on to some other idea. Early on, they decide how much they are willing to invest or lose, and if their experimentation exceeds that, they usually end it. Enterprising families manage their risks by using this insight about testing actions early, inexpensively, and quickly to manage their risks. They look at what skills their enterprise has, the people in and out of the organization who might be interested in joining, and the resources that could be made available to pursue something new.

Steps to Promote Ambidexterity in Preservation and Innovation

It is easier for an organization to support innovation when the following design elements are used and aligned. Enterprising families tend to use several means to encourage entrepreneurial action through its levels while managing risk taking. Of course the choice of which one(s) will be most suitable for your enterprise will depend on its size, age, and complexity. But some combination of ideas discussed here will help you to carve unique design features for your enterprise.

- Creating and renewing formal structures
- Number and nature of innovations
- Idea generation by kin and nonkin
- Family enterprise incubator
- Expanding networks and alliances

Creating and renewing formal structures. In chapter 4, we explained that as a family grows, it can be helpful to create more formalized family structures to help preserve family commitment, resolve difficult dilemmas, and enable family participation and possible entrepreneurial activity. Since the late 1980s, family business experts like John Ward have observed in their classic books[7] the significant positive impact of creating formal governance and accountability structures as the numbers and the complexity of the controlling family and its enterprises increased. Successful enterprising families work hard to develop structures that help to build accountability and discipline in their organizations.

Nevertheless, no one permanent, universal governance structure works equally effectively for accomplishing this task.[8] Which governance structures to establish and the time to create them vary, depending on how diversified the family business has become and how many family members across the generations are working in or are interested in working in the business(es). Group Park Avenue is a family enterprise founded by Norman D. Hébert in 1959 when he acquired a Chevrolet dealership in Montreal that was on the verge of bankruptcy. His son, Norman E. Hébert Jr., joined in 1981. The father-son duo worked together for ten years, after which the father passed the

> *Through a cycle of acting quickly, learning,*
> *reshaping current activities into new action,*
> *relearning, and deciding in advance*
> *what losses are the limit, the enterprising family*
> *can tackle the unknown.*

leadership to his son, who bought the shares from his parents slowly over time. The third generation joined in 2013. Fifty-five years after founding a business with 670 employees and twenty car dealerships across Canada, this enterprising family has been innovating and growing. Norman Hébert Jr. explained that while theirs was a small family with two siblings in every generation, only one of whom worked in the leadership role, they found it useful to set up regular facilitated family meetings to make sure there was a formalized pathway for members of different generations to communicate. In addition, their active advisory board, with independent-minded successful individuals from the community, helped bring accountability and discipline to the enterprise, without which it would have been difficult to innovate and grow over generations.

While Park Avenue is a relatively young enterprise with a bean pole (long and thin) family structure, it is useful to look at a multigenerational company that has and continues to wrestle with the process of forming a corporate governance structure that enables the entrepreneurial tradition to continue. The Pantaleón Group of Guatemala was founded in 1849. Today, it is a conglomerate with businesses in sugar, real estate, and finance; over 140 family members are involved in the enterprise. There have been four generations of strong, family patriarchal leadership, all of them entrepreneurial except for the third generation, and at last report they have explored moving to a more shared leadership model. In the meantime, in the view of the researchers from the Central American business school INCAE who studied the company, "innovative capacity is hard-wired in the structure of Pantaleón Sugar Holdings, where a new project and strategy unit encourages new ideas, and where there is a team of nonfamily professionals who are strongly encouraged to develop new ideas or to adapt ideas from Colombia, Brazil, or Australia."[9] Learning from best practices in other companies and countries is a long tradition. Considerable initiative is encouraged, as long as agreed-on strategy is followed, and projects often only need budget approval to get underway.

In an effort to retain more effective nonfamily members in the business, only two family members are in executive positions, and no more will be allowed. In fact, a large number of other extended family members are not owners of the business or in contact with those who are. The current governance structure was created with the help of outside consultants and ten family members attending a Northwestern University family business program. There is a shareholders assembly, a family assembly (with the same membership as the shareholders assembly, except that spouses are invited to social events), a family council, and a family office. On the business side, there is a board of directors of the holding company along with boards of directors for each of the operating companies. Relationships between family board members and nonfamily professional managers are characterized as "nose in–hands off," creating a relatively flat, empowered culture. Instituting a more formal governance structure does not seem to be hurting the innovative capacity of the business; rather, it is increasing the likelihood that the long-standing entrepreneurial spirit can continue across generations.

Dabur is a property development company and one of several controlled by the five-generation-old Burman family in India, having started in 1884 as an ayurvedic medicine company. It is an example of the family moving out of operations completely and limiting their involvement only to strategy and governance. They discovered—after considerable family turmoil and resistance—that this led to much better growth and profitability.[10] Currently seven of eleven Dabur Directors are Burman family members. The Burman family constitution does not allow family members to be employed in the flagship company. As a consequence, family members have become entrepreneurs and investors in new ventures, while ensuring professional management of the main business.

As the companies and their families evolve over time, the governance structures must also be reexamined and renewed. Ritter, a fifth-generation agribusiness and communications company founded in 1906 in Arkansas, has been addressing the renewal of its formal board. Concerned because there was too little turnover of family and nonfamily board members, the chairman and former CEO launched discussion of board policies for membership. At first, board members did not show interest in term or age limits. But individual and peer director evaluations were introduced at the behest of an independent board member. Her mention of her own retirement prompted the board to begin thinking about what kind of experience a new director should have. That led to measures to establish qualification criteria and a formal nominating process. Over a seven-year period, the board has elected one new independent director and two family member directors, allowing for new energy and ideas.[11]

The Spanish Pharma company mentioned in the last chapter provides another nuanced take on professionalization that attempts to make efficient what can be routinized and retain creativity where it is needed. More than succession in general from family members to outsiders, it involves differing ownership and styles of decision-making in three realms: administrative, operational, and strategic. They assume that each realm, in order, requires increasing numbers of decisions about uncertainty, where less is known about likely outcomes. Therefore family members retain the decisions where the most intuitive skills are required. The greater the number of unknowns about the decision, the more intuitive skills will be needed, and the move towards formalizing processes based on analytical work will necessarily be slower.[12] In our view, their process might overstate the desirability of eliminating appropriate intuition in making administrative and operational decisions. While greater use of analytical materials and formality there is likely and appropriate, change needs to be driven by entrepreneurial intuition even in those areas. It might also overstate

As the companies and their families evolve over time, the governance structures must also be reexamined and renewed.

the exclusive capacity of this family for making decisions under uncertainty, but it is an attempt to determine how the family can bring in more nonfamily members into the leadership roles at all levels of the enterprise. Furthermore, family members are also getting trained professionally to handle various levels of leadership.[13] As a result, the family has moved through the first three heirs in family succession to more educated members of the fourth and fifth generations and has allowed administrative professionalization to support leadership by a more trained heir. Then it used a board of advisors instead of the more formal board of directors, but has now transitioned to a formal board of directors. The ultimate step in their march toward formalization and professionalization culminated in allowing even the most uncertain strategic decisions to be handled by a nonfamily CEO. Nevertheless, the family is keeping a close watch to determine whether this otherwise capable CEO has sufficient entrepreneurial spirit. It can take time to get the balance right.

The Hemas group of Sri Lanka, a third-generation family business established in 1948, took early steps to institutionalize entrepreneurship and governance. Consequently the family professionalized the board and appointed a nonfamily chairman of the board. After a few years, the family appointed a nonfamily group CEO while retaining the youngest family member as the head of the hospital business. Other family members who are above fifty-five moved out of operations and passed over all entrepreneurial initiatives within the existing businesses to nonfamily professionals. There are currently four family members on the board and seven nonfamily directors.

Not all formalization of governance automatically leads to new entrepreneurial behavior. W. J. Towell & Co. is a successful fifth-generation conglomerate founded in 1866 with headquarters in Muscat, Oman. It worked very hard in recent years to address the increasing complexity of its business by restructuring into seven homogeneous clusters of businesses, each with its own board of family directors, including directors from the main company holding board, the cluster CEO, and the cluster CFO. This arrangement has begun to work quite effectively, with considerable decision-making delegated to each cluster board, though control remains with the holding board. The restructuring improved management of the company and family complexity (with over 150 family members involved), increased transparency and communication of actions, produced greater equality among family members' private lifestyles, and reduced private use of group-owned assets. The company continues to work on other improvements to its governance structure; nevertheless, since the business provides the income of many family members, the structure has been designed to *reduce* unnecessary risks, not create more entrepreneurial initiative. Through clarity about the roles of the cluster board and the main holdings board, clear limits to decision-making capacity, and strong engagement of family board members in the board of each cluster, caution and stability are ensured, as is desired.[14]

Number and nature of innovations. Most healthy firms make continual small investments in building their core business so they can sustain product quality, understand target customers, assure sufficient supplies, maintain competitive pricing, and so on. While these incremental innovations are individually not dramatic, they add up over time. That can be sufficient to maintain the enterprise and a vast improvement over settling for status quo, particularly if the enterprise is not in a rapidly changing competitive setting and the family system is not going through major evolutions. But if that is all an enterprise does, in the long term it could be difficult to see and develop the entrepreneurial opportunities ultimately necessary for survival and growth.

Enterprising families constantly explore other possibilities, making "side bets" that can be either the beginnings of a great long-term success or relatively inexpensive opportunities to learn what not to do. The side bets can be progressive innovations in nature. Examples include probes into related but different businesses, areas of deep interest and knowledge on the part of particular family members (or other organizational members), trial expansions into new geographies, acquisitions of undeveloped products or small companies, or places to try out the abilities of family members who feel confined by the existing core. A telling example of managing a side bet can be seen in the Garcia Tuñon company of Venezuela, which for two generations had specialized in a General Motors dealership through considerable economic and political turbulence. A third-generation member wanted to continue the dealership and related businesses but also to diversify away from the car industry without incurring too much reputational risk. So while managing and growing the core business, he tinkered with Internet-based business opportunities but kept these explorations away from the company brand to preserve the legacy in case they did not work.[15]

Taking a page from the mind-set of venture capitalists and portfolio managers, enterprising families spread the risk. They know that unproven ideas have a low probability of success but also the potential for very high returns. Thus the need to accept the inherent uncertainty is offset by diversified investments. Interestingly, Pantaleón (mentioned earlier) has taken a managed approach to risks. As the executive responsible for special projects noted that being first to innovate carries some risks, Pantaleón balances the risk of innovation with in-depth study of new projects. Projects supported by sound analysis are undertaken. He adds, "Co-generation was a risky venture at the time it was done, dependent on a government-regulated entity and on a new technology, but the project went ahead because deep analysis had been done." Pantaleón also reduces risk by maintaining a balanced portfolio that includes some relatively low-risk investments, for example, ones in real estate. Still another way that the company manages risk is by bringing reputable investors or partners such as the World Bank's IFC on board, as it did in the case of its Brazilian venture. The IFC invested because "we had done our homework. A lot has to do with the quality of the human resources that this company has. There are good technical people." Another example of risk reduction through the involvement of knowledgeable partners was its investment in the candy business, a new business for Pantaleón done in alliance with a successful Colombian candy manufacturer, Colombina.[16] This is a wonderful example of ambidextrous entrepreneurial thinking. Part of the portfolio provides steady and relatively safe returns in order to offset riskier and more profitable investments. Partners are also used to spread the risk. Another portion is reserved for small uncertain investments that can turn into something larger.

Enterprising families constantly explore other possibilities, making "side bets" that can be either the beginnings of a great long-term success or relatively inexpensive opportunities to learn what not to do.

Idea generation by kin and nonkin. Enterprising families create a climate where even ideas that seem "far out" are welcomed and seriously considered. This is easier said than done because senior people involved with the core business often already feel overloaded, deeply schooled in the ways of the existing core, and reluctant to "waste time" on anything that is very different from what they know works and about which they have relative certainty. On the other hand, part of the advantage of the family business is that existing resources, skills, and connections can readily be tapped if early market responses demonstrate that an idea is worth pursuing. This calls for walking a fine line between total separation from and total containment to the evaluation process for new ideas.

Family organizations can be more informal in inviting ideas and proposals, if there is some tradition of using entrepreneurial shifts successfully. This is illustrated by the history of the Menasha companies, which was introduced earlier and is discussed in detail below. And where there is a tradition of encouraging bold failures, as at Michelin, discussed in chapter 5, amazing things can happen. Here is a striking example from the Millers' outstanding research on Michelin. Years ago, a team tried to build a rubber rail-tire for trains. It flopped badly in its test. "Boss Edouard Michelin Sr. immediately summoned the hapless development team to his office. They fully expected a reprimand. Instead they were effusively congratulated for their daring. And Edouard gave the team more funds to perfect their system. Decades later it is still useful in developing countries."[17] However, it is harder to make this informal process effective in a punitive, top-down driven culture, where a founder or successor has made all the entrepreneurial decisions and often personally come up with the entrepreneurial ideas that are adapted. In fact, the more brilliant and innovative the founder or top management has been, the more discipline and self-restraint they must display to create encouragement for younger organizational members.

In a paradox of power, less powerful people dealing with them tend to hold back. When they appear "weak" and not ready for more responsibility, they are not taken as seriously as they may deserve.[18] Enterprising families break such hierarchical barriers by working with a consultant or by creating or working with a board that has some strong outsiders. For example, consider Chandran Menon of Kolhapur, India, the CEO of Menon and Menon Ltd and its founder, along with his younger brother. A brilliant and dynamic entrepreneur, inventor, and self-taught engineer, Menon recognized that managing a company wasn't the same as creating one, and he was determined to learn how to be an extraordinary manager also. He decided to run an executive development retreat, and he worked through a Peace Corps consultant who had been helping him to hire a visiting American consultant and a young, inexperienced colleague we will call "Mollie" as facilitators. Early in the workshop, small task groups went off to work on assignments. They returned, and the first group was barely two minutes into their report when Menon—who wanted to correct an assumption they'd made—burst in to tell them how wrong they were. His outburst resulted in complete silence. Mollie[19] finally replied, "I wasn't particularly committed to this idea when we discussed it in our group. But you were just so rude and insulting that now I want to defend the idea fiercely." This stunned Menon into silence. After a few awkward moments, with welling tears, he confessed, "I had no idea. Will you please all forgive me?" Menon later marked that moment in his official biography as a turning point in the evolution of his own leadership. At that point he stopped allowing his brilliance and dynamism—the very qualities that led to his disproportionate power—to inhibit others.[20]

In another example, Hema Hattangady, CEO of Conzerv in India, was the daughter-in-law of the founder. She had been put in charge when a powerful investor and board member saw that the father-in-law was not doing a good job of running the energy meter company. Her husband remained the chief technical person. She turned out to be an innovative though non-technical leader who overcame extraordinary obstacles, including constant ridicule and undermining from her father-in-law, to build the company. But after five very successful years problems arose, including complacency and arrogance among the top team. With support from the powerful board member who had been her mentor, she decided to attend a Harvard executive education program. There she realized that she had been so busy innovating and trying to compete in a difficult and sometimes corrupt economy that she had not listened to or encouraged the younger managers in the company enough. She held a series of meetings with most of her staff, later explaining that she looked them in the eye and said, "When you try to come to me with ideas, I've been telling you that we know it all. We've got it all. Well, I set a terrible example. Why didn't anyone come and tell me that I was behaving like this?" They said, "We tried to, you just wouldn't listen." Her openness in admitting her flaws and a genuine desire to change just melted people.[21] She then introduced a culture change program, which led to much greater initiatives from below and another organizational transformation. To finance growth, and for personal reasons, the company was sold to Schneider, and she and her husband have continued with the public company.

Sometimes barriers are broken only with a successful rebellion by a younger family member, either leading an internal coup or going outside to start something new and bringing it back inside the company once it is successful. When this works it can be very effective, but it is a risky way to proceed.

Incremental innovations often provide a good starting point for members of the rising generation to build entrepreneurial skills. By experimenting with incremental innovations within their current jobs, members of the younger generation can try new methods or procedures to make some improvements and efficiencies. Not only does taking such small steps help to build confidence, it also gives them a reason to discuss such small wins with other family and nonfamily members in the enterprise, thereby gaining legitimacy. More often than not, the seeds of progressive extensions as well as radical innovations are scattered throughout the organization, mostly lying dormant because of the time and resources required to excel in core operations. Building on these smaller innovations within the enterprise is a great way to work on a new product, a new business opportunity, or a new core methodology to open a new market. Treating it as an experiment and testing its feasibility along the way helps those running it to learn and grow. The alternate approach that some members of the next generation try to adopt (showing the senior management how old and outmoded their ways are) is usually ineffective. The desire for next-generation members to prove themselves often gets in the way of staying humble and exploratory; this inadvertently increases opposition and the likelihood of being treated as not ready for real responsibility.

Enterprising families around the world tend to buy into the argument that like driving, entrepreneurship is a skill that is developed only by "sitting behind the wheel." Doing is essential to learning, and making mistakes is part of the learning process. They focus on thinking of the best ways to allow the requisite hands-on learning while finding methods to limit the size of mistakes and their impact on the core operations. Having several small experiments going on to spread risk and limit losses tends to work for even conservative families.

Resistance to innovation, of course, can come from below, not just above. For example, consider the next-generation sons of the founder parents of MSI, the Brunt family building supply business in the Virgin Islands. They worried that their free-wheeling, creative architect father was not conservative enough and might put the business in jeopardy, leaving them without alternative sources of income or alternative business experience. The opportunistic acquisition of a cement company which the sons could run as a "side business," quite profitably as it turned out, helped to hedge the bet in a satisfying way.[22]

One of the ironies of families is that members know each other incredibly well; while this allows for unique understanding, it sometimes skews or limits members' views, which are based on behaviors in earlier stages of life rather than current capabilities and interests. The nature of role relationships ensures that when a person is treated according to a known role (such as a child or a sibling), it often pulls that predefined and somewhat constrained behavior from that person, and this in turn "confirms" the skewed view. This cycle can make it hard to escape from self-reinforcing mind-sets. When this happens, both parties can feel frustrated or stalemated and retreat into hopelessness about "working with family members." But either party can break the pattern by pointing it out, noting how the behavior of each person elicits the exact behavior in the other that reinforces the undesirable behavior; once this happens they can explore ways around the pattern. Sometimes a neutral friend, relative, or trained expert can help both parties see the pattern more objectively so they can step back and find ways to develop more productive interactions. Collaboration among generations, siblings, cousins, and involved relatives will be desirable in promoting entrepreneurial initiative, as is the case in successful enterprising families.

The Paragon Footwear group in India, founded in 1975, has evolved a model that encourages entrepreneurial ideas from any family member. All such ideas are initially considered by the Family Business Board for piloting before institutionalizing as a new division. Since members of the next generation also attend the board meeting as invitees, a family culture of entrepreneurship is encouraged and sustained.

> *Enterprising families around the world*
> *tend to buy into the argument that like driving,*
> *entrepreneurship is a skill that is developed*
> *only by "sitting behind the wheel."*

Family enterprise incubator. Some organizations create venture funds staffed by family members who are responsive to new ideas or by expert outsiders whose judgment is trusted. A few big nonfamily public companies have made this work, though often when a senior executive introduces the venture fund concept, it tends to fade when that senior executive moves on. With their long tenures and cross-generational orientation, enterprising families have a distinct advantage in making this idea work. In chapter 5 we mentioned radical or breakthrough innovations, which usually start with completely different customer segments and create an entirely new industry or product category. Perhaps a son or daughter, niece or nephew, or the bright offspring of an employee who has recently graduated from engineering or business school has an idea that would be too radical for a big company. It might be worth giving or loaning that person some modest resources to test whether some people would indeed pay for something new and different and whether the idea might be profitable if it didn't have to carry the usual company overhead.

Obviously the enterprise will want to pursue only those ventures that seem promising, but it is quite difficult to judge which ones will be successful compared to activities that are natural incremental expansions of the core business and its practices. Therefore, it is prudent to have several "extreme experiments" going at once. These provide quick tests of market interest or technical possibility at modest expenditure and give the business and family a sense of the total amount to risk on potential high payoffs with longer odds. How much the enterprise is willing to risk depends on the stage and life cycle of the enterprise and family members, along with the impact of potential losses. No one likes losses or failures, but since some are inevitable if you do anything new and different, putting limits on the total you are willing to risk makes it easier to experiment.

Two more examples of generating and vetting entrepreneurial ideas from family businesses follow.

Popular Automobiles is a large, diversified Indian family business founded in 1940, with two second-generation and one third-generation member involved. It decided to limit entry of any new family member into their core business (automobile dealerships and spare parts distribution) to avoid overcrowding. Instead, the business started to encourage interested family members to come up with new entrepreneurial ideas for incubation and funding by the family. As a result, the daughter of a director, a musician with an MBA from a top US business school, came up with the idea of setting up a new business to teach instrumental music, received funding, and successfully launched it.

A large, diversified third-generation family business in India has a structured screening process for new venture ideas. The five senior family members have entrusted the responsibility to screen and mentor new ideas of next-generation members to their two cousins who are professionally educated. They have a two-level filtering process: a one-page project proposal and a detailed business plan. The two cousins keep reporting to the other cousins on progress.

Similarly, some business families are beginning to experiment with systematic ways to have next generation family and nonfamily members present their business plans and ideas to a panel of "family venture capitalists," bringing inside what might be called family venturing. When these experiments are part of the family enterprise, they can preserve the accountability and discipline of the ongoing businesses, yet incubate entrepreneurial opportunities. They pay attention to structural arrangements to avoid messing up the core business without choking off all higher risk opportunities before they get close to full exploitation, all with minimum losses.

The initiative to incubate new ventures within a family enterprise is certainly not the exclusive purview of the leaders of the senior generation. At times, siblings or cousins may band together to cocreate new initiatives either under the rubric of their family business or outside it, while still keeping family relationships going.

Family venturing necessitates some discussion around the following questions: Will the new ventures be fully spun off or brought back in when proven viable? Who will get the profits, if any? Will those who get involved risk their salaries, regular jobs, family shares, or other opportunities? Will they be allowed to earn their way back in? Will there be any penalties for honest, hard-working failures? How long will any experiments be allowed to continue? How will they be evaluated? Cash flow? Profitability? Learning opportunities? Are there positions for family members who do not otherwise fit?[23] Protecting against competition? There may not be universally correct answers to these questions, but enterprising families make it their responsibility to discuss them and at least partly determine in advance the process by which such questions will be answered. Often family structures such as family meetings or councils are used, but decisions don't necessarily have to be based within such structures. It is more critical to ensure that there is a well-understood way to make these decisions before any serious conflicts or family rifts arise.

Expanding networks and alliances. Family enterprises tend to feel more comfortable working with other family enterprises. The company of Patricia Ghany, the second-generation leader of Esau Oilfield

Supplies Company of Trinidad and Tobago, has always been a one-stop shop for all that is needed to build oil platforms. While the company has three main product lines, it often collaborates with similar family businesses that are led by the second generation leadership, as it is easier to relate with them and form strong relationships. In her words:

> **We started building collaborations to go about the expansion. … Mostly, the firms we were interested in were also family businesses that like us were going over into the second generation. Finding the typical family-ownership traits in common helped greatly in establishing a good relationship. We realized we are all facing similar issues.**[24]

Not only do such collaborations help diffuse the risk, they also help nurture entrepreneurial ideas and networks. Choosing partners or companies for alliances has its own set of risks, so the process requires careful selection, but creative linkages can have great benefits. For example, the Surber family led ATF, Inc., a Chicago suburb–based manufacturer of fasteners and other customized components for a number of sectors in a highly competitive industry. Recognizing that ATF, although successful, was not large enough to compete on a global basis, Don Surber launched The Global Fastener Alliance, a group of nine family companies around the world that shared practices, licensing arrangements, joint ventures, family member internship opportunities, and (when appropriate) manufacturing capacity.[25] The alliance gave the business sufficient size and scope to compete in this capital-intensive industry with much larger, publicly traded global competitors. In addition to the direct business benefits of this collaboration, it became possible for family members of the younger generation to work at the company of one of the other alliance members, gaining appropriate industry experience while working outside of their own family company for a while. For example, the son of a German member company, EJOT, worked at ATF for over a year and grew close to the family. Eventually, Don's son and the young German created two manufacturing joint ventures, one in the United States and one in Mexico. Arrangements like this provide a creative way of developing younger family members while reducing the probability that they will feel stifled if they work directly in the family company before gaining outside experience. While ATF used the alliance peer network structure to broaden its reach, twelve leading multigenerational wine families of Australia formed an alliance[26] in 2009 to educate the world about the premium wines of Australia. Regular networking and educational events help to bring these enterprising families together and inevitably lead to the generation of new ideas and opportunities to benefit the alliance members.

As we have emphasized in our discussions about the necessity for ambidexterity, different skills and judgments are required for sustaining existing business and venturing into activities that do not have easily predictable and known outcomes. One critical challenge is to

Some business families are beginning to experiment with systematic ways to have next generation family and nonfamily members present their business plans and ideas to a panel of "family venture capitalists."

think about how to quickly test and learn from venturing into the new and unknown. Even for projects that will be long-term breakthrough efforts if successful, like the Michelin radial tire or Corning glass fiber, the idea is to make as explicit as possible the assumptions behind a proposal and devise tests that quickly determine whether the assumptions are correct, or at least eliminate ones that are incorrect. Will anyone actually want to buy the "great" new product? Will they pay enough to make the requisite investment worthwhile? Is there a vast new potential market without competitors if you can succeed in creating the product or service? Is it actually feasible to make it? How can it be distributed to potential customers at a reasonable cost?

Can it be sold by your existing sales mechanisms? And if the idea is not a product or business but a new process or a first-time service, what assumptions are being made in order to make it worth doing?

To illustrate many of the points in this chapter and throughout the book and their interconnections, we now include extensive descriptions of two disparate organizations that have managed to be entrepreneurial and innovative for a long time and are consciously ambidextrous in pursuing opportunities while sustaining core business. One is the Menasha Companies in the United States, in its fifth generation of family ownership and going strong, while the other is Corona, founded in 1881 in Colombia, which is testing radical innovation in a new division (Nexentia) while successfully maintaining its construction materials business and big-box home-improvement stores.

Innovation through Five Generations: Menasha Corporation[27]

Founded in 1852 as a dry goods retailing company, this family enterprise has evolved from manufacturing wooden tubs and containers, through owning, managing, and selling timberlands into brown corrugated box production, to promotional displays and now consumer packaging created using their close knowledge of large retailers to work with consumer goods manufacturers. While today a billion-dollar enterprise, it had its ups and downs over the years. At every turn, however, it developed entrepreneurial solutions that have allowed the company to survive and thrive.

A number of company—and family—features have created and allowed for entrepreneurial initiative across generations. From its earliest days the company has utilized "outsiders" in critical ways. The founder, Elisha D. Smith, had come to Menasha, Wisconsin, from Rhode Island in 1850 to partner in a dry goods store. However, shortly after he arrived he saw an opportunity in a struggling pail factory; borrowing money from his father-in-law, he bought the business. Twenty years later, it was the largest woodenware manufacturer in the Midwest. However, despite the continued high volume of orders, costs were not contained, so in 1872 the company had to shut down because it couldn't pay its suppliers or employees. While it reopened in receivership shortly thereafter, in 1875 Elisha incorporated under the name Menasha Wooden Ware Company, turning once more to his father-in-law, who agreed to help out. However, he would own 90 percent of the shares, his daughter 2 percent, and Elisha none. He also insisted that Elisha bring in a new, nonfamily president (8% shares) and work as a salaried general superintendent. It took Elisha nine years to regain the presidency and eventually buy the shares back from his father-in-law.

Elisha's rebellious son Charles declared he did not want to go to college but after three months as a lumberjack decided to go to Princeton. Afterwards he started his own business making broom handles and barrels. During the next twenty years he built it successfully while also serving as treasurer for Menasha Wooden Ware Co., until his company was bought by Menasha. Charles then saw opportunity in acquiring, managing, and selling timberland, which turned out to be a thriving part of the larger company. When Charles died prematurely, however, a nonfamily member was chosen to run the overall company—but he only lasted twenty-six months.

Charles's son Mowry suggested to a new nonfamily president that there was opportunity in making corrugated boxes. The president resisted but was ousted by the family-dominated board, and he was succeeded by two nonfamily presidents who were excellent stewards

Regular networking and educational events

help to bring these enterprising families together

and inevitably lead to the generation of

new ideas and opportunities to benefit

the alliance members.

of the company, improving manufacturing operations and instituting cost controls. Meanwhile, the next generation became heavily involved in innovation regarding the last of the Wooden Ware products and ultimately moved into corrugated box making. Taking advantage of the different skills of two brothers, the company was split into two, one focusing on manufacturing and marketing products with the other managing a portfolio of stocks. Over time each contributed considerably to the company—and family—wealth.

Noting that plastics were becoming a threat to paper packaging led to another entrepreneurial move: the acquisition of a company that had transitioned from woodenware into plastic containers. That original acquisition has developed into half of the current company.

After Mowry retired, he was succeeded by another nonfamily CEO because Mowry believed that no member of the next generation was ready to run the company. This CEO was conservative and worked on professionalizing the board and the company's processes, including bringing in talented nonfamily managers. He saw the need to provide liquidity to the shareholders and created a liquidity event, indicating he had the complete confidence of the family.

After twenty years of nonfamily leadership, Menasha Corporation returned the reins to a fourth-generation family member. Using debt for the first time, he drove major growth, diversifying and decentralizing the company. Introducing a team approach, he gave considerable autonomy to the companies that were acquired, encouraging entrepreneurial behavior and close attention to customer needs. One of his acquisitions in commercial printing and promotional materials gave the company its first exposure to the consumer products market, which eventually, under a fifth-generation leader of Menasha Packaging, led to the next transformative idea, the Retail Integration Institute (RII).

This marketing innovation demonstrates how the Menasha culture promoted and supported successful innovations. It was developed by a self-organized and self-managed team of sales, marketing, and design people from different plants with different functions. It targeted big-box stores to gain a deeper understanding of what types of packaging and promotional displays were most effective, then it used this knowledge to sell packaging solutions to consumer product companies. Along with attaining leadership in sustainable packaging, this has proved highly successful.

Details of this story illustrate some of the innovation-enabling traditions of the company. The initiative contributed to the rebranding of Menasha Packaging. Though known as a business-to-business brown box manufacturer, the company decided it should focus more on packaging for consumer packaged goods companies (CPGs). But the problem was that they didn't know the "retail language." So they set out to learn about retail. In the process they realized that other packagers really didn't know the retail market any more than Menasha did, so they began to leverage their newly acquired knowledge in the marketplace—becoming the retail experts for Walmart and Walgreens in particular. They went to the CPGs with information that even the retailers didn't have about floor displays. The RII group, which was considered just a marketing group, became something much more. They took on the brand and went to market as RII, not Menasha Packaging. They knew that they needed to separate themselves from Menasha Packaging, the brown box company that had been around for 150 years and had recently been up for sale. So they made sales calls and went to retail trade shows as RII.

At the booth where Menasha Packaging products were showcased, the branding banners read Retail Integration Institute, and then in smaller type, "serviced by Menasha Packaging." That, in itself, was innovative. But what is quintessentially Menasha is that they did this without clearing it with the CEO of Menasha Packaging. He found out when he saw the booth. It was all about RII, not Menasha Packaging. But he let them do it. According to Jeff Krepline, a long-term employee who was there at the time, the CEO smiled and said, "I know what you guys are doing." And they continued to do it for five years, ultimately elevating the Menasha Packaging brand and changing its perception in the marketplace. Chances are if they had gone to the CEO and asked if they could go to market with the RII brand, barely mentioning MP, he probably would have said "no." But they wanted to show him. When he came to that trade show, the RII booth was packed and that was proof that they had made a shrewd and innovative decision. They didn't worry about doing this without clearing it with him. They knew that they would have his support and that he wouldn't punish them for not sharing their strategy ahead of time.

Throughout Menasha's history, employees had been empowered, encouraged, and motivated to implement innovations at all levels in the company—design, sales, manufacturing, and internal systems—and to do so continuously. The expectation is "continuous improvement"—innovation. There is a strong training program in which the excellence process is taught, involving innovation and experimentation.

Sustaining innovation is never easy, and the more that an innovation differs from existing ways of doing things—products, markets, techniques, processes, required skills and so on, the greater will be the need for mastering ambidexterity.

Leadership is the other factor that has had an impact on the culture of innovation at Menasha. Once again, the expectation is that the leaders will support innovation financially but also allow time for an innovation to be successful (an advantage of being privately held). While Menasha as a corporation doesn't tend to take big risks, risk taking among employees is encouraged. The understanding is that if you aren't constantly experimenting and trying new things, you aren't doing your job. But many experiments fail, and that is also acceptable as long as the lessons learned are clearly articulated. Menasha leaders are also willing to get down in the trenches and provide support wherever it is needed. They are "hands on" but not micromanaging leaders. Innovative employees are recognized and celebrated to other employees. Employees are encouraged to communicate between businesses and among each other, learning how innovative practices or products in one area can be utilized in another. Open communication is practiced and reinforced.

Jeff Krepline claimed that "the level of engagement from the leadership team is what makes Menasha who we are. They are totally unbelievable. They make everything personal. It's really not just about doing your job. It's about working together to create something special—and everyone is in it together. And that goes back twenty-five years. I came to a dinner right after joining the company, just out of college. I was sitting at a table at the beginning of the evening having a great conversation with some gentleman sitting next to me. When the evening got under way, I realized that that gentleman was the CEO."

Another fifth-generation innovation that is proving to be useful is the creation of the Smith Family Council, aimed at improving communications between the business, board, and other family members. With over 150 family shareholders, this structure is a necessary component allowing for future entrepreneurial decisions related to issues such as major investment, dividend policy, liquidity options, family member roles in and out of the business, and so on.

The history and organizational mechanisms contributing to entrepreneurial behavior throughout the Menasha Company. Looking at the history of encouraging entrepreneurial behavior, we can see many of the universal elements of organizations that encourage innovation and some others particular to family business:

- *A vision of innovation.* The company self identifies as having been innovative from the beginning. The company tagline connected to its vision is "Menasha Corporation encourages its employees to pursue innovation every day." Jim Kotek, current CEO, talks about propagating the vision that everyone is expected to contribute to innovation at all levels as part of their jobs. He tries to connect what they are doing to the company mission, vision, and strategy.

- *Ingrained flexibility.* Right from the beginning there was not an ironfisted founder, ruling from above. Deposed by his father-in-law and replaced by a nonfamily member CEO for ten years, the founder had to buy back the shares. Over the years, nonfamily members were brought in to run things as perceived to be needed, and family members were put in charge when it was believed they were ready and able.

- *Early professionalization of the board.* This provided support for the idea that in order to survive, the organization would have to adapt from time to time, which it did.

- *Early commitment to empowering teams to run businesses and projects.* Because a number of acquisitions were made in technologies or segments where the family did not have particular expertise, they were willing to rely on others and to pull together those with particular knowledge, family or not, to figure out how to do things.

- *An informal culture in which no one was afraid to speak up to senior people and had easy access.* First of all, plenty of major decisions made by family members had not proved to be right and had to be reversed. Secondly, some of the best ideas, such as getting very close to retailers, came from below in the organization and were then approved and supported by the family. As family member Sylvia Shepherd (the source for much of this information) put it, "There is no feeling at any level of a glass ceiling. You need a company culture that anyone can rise to the top. There is not a lot of hierarchy, so a salesman can talk to the CEO about something interesting he heard from a customer. There is not a formal process, with lots of proposals, presentations, large numbers of procedures—in a week we can get moving. There are forms for projections, but not as elaborate as many big companies. It is a more streamlined process, anyone can do it." There is a general aversion to rules and restriction.

- *People are rewarded for good ideas* and not punished for honest mistakes.

- *Experimentation expected, with an understanding that experiments fail but that lessons learned must be articulated.*

- *Family members wanting to work in the business or within it were expected to prove themselves.* For example, in 1980 the board decided that after twenty years of a nonfamily member CEO, they wanted family leadership again. They weren't sure which of two family cousins to choose, for one had operating experience and the other finance expertise. When the board chose Tad Shepherd (operating experience), he was directed to get an executive MBA, and then he would be given a year to prove he could run the company. They told him that "if we feel there is a problem, we will look for someone else." Currently, there are no written employment policies for family members; the HR department is trusted to act on the basis of competence, not family status. Family members are considered to be just like anyone else.

- *No formal shareholder agreement.* For the most part, shares were just passed down through the generations; some went out of the family to a second-generation marriage partner, but not enough to give anyone else control. The family just worked things out.

- *Culture of hands-on support from leadership, yet not micromanaging.* Leaders just jump in when needed but don't overcontrol.

- *Making it "personal."* Top managers do not keep employees at arms-length but rather treat them as fully worthy individuals.

Not every company is fortunate enough to have a history that supports flexibility, initiative from below, willingness to try new things, experience leading to an understanding that the family is not the sole possessor of knowledge and good ideas, and decentralization and reliance on teams, but this one serves as a vivid example of what is possible when the mechanisms can be established and accepted. Are any ideas in this case story useful for your enterprising family?

The Complexities of Ambidexterity and Innovation

Our final example is a Colombian company with a long tradition of innovation and a perceived need for more radical innovation with uncertain outcomes. Alexis Sabet Echavarría, a fourth-generation member of the family who has been in an operating position in the business for only five years, described his experiences as follows.

The company began around 1900 with imported textiles and then began to manufacture textiles. Next it acquired a nearly bankrupt ceramics and glass producer and infused it with technology to manufacture ceramics. From ceramics came the diversification into construction under the Corona brand. Mining followed next, with the extraction of nonmetallic minerals. The founder died young, but his sons continued the entrepreneurial tradition by creating successful new businesses in sanitary wares, tiles, paints, home improvement retail stores, and specialized kitchen and bath stores, with a minority stake in department stores and a bank. Many of these businesses were built with strategic partners. In the 1990s, as the Colombian economy became more competitive. Alexis Sabet Echavarría felt that more innovation was necessary to accelerate growth.

> By 2020 how could we *multiply* revenues? Organic growth would not be sufficient. How could we implement open innovation? We began implementing an innovation strategy, from adding new business, acquisitions, and ultimately open innovation. To do open innovation we had to create a separate internal nanotech startup we called Nexentia, always leveraging what we know. What can we do with nonmetallic minerals like kaolin, calcium carbonate, and silica, so that construction, pharma, food, paint, or agricultural industries can get added value? How can we improve our advantage?
>
> Now, one tech line, using techniques in micro encapsulation with non-metallic minerals, is very innovative—few are doing it. We are also pursuing using nanoparticles. What functionalities can we build in to calcium? We know little about the other industries; what capabilities do we build in, how do we scale up, like an experiment?

Managing High Uncertainty

> We are doing creation at Nexentia. We have some results. Corona declared 3–4 percent of revenue for research and development including Nexentia, because it is dealing in high

uncertainty. We are still learning about the potential of these technologies. We are making long-term bets, [and] still don't know who our customers are, [or] what treatments will work. The first bets are early clinical studies, like microencapsulating natural extracts for the agro industry.

As we narrow the uncertainty gap with our findings, and get positive results, we have to be willing to invest more than what we had budgeted earlier. There has to be a deliverable, make new bets at each stage. We have to stop and decide whether we are willing to make the next investment. We are collaborating with a Colombian research university in entrepreneurship, and there is a vital entrepreneurial ecosystem in Medellin. We are becoming a model for how to collaborate with a university.

Internal Resistance
It isn't easy; there are very important internal hurdles in building Nexentia into a company: five years ago, at the beginning of this project, I was alone; I was the only full-time employee, and a part-time cross-functional team was appointed to help support the project. Employees investing part-time have a hard time committing to the project, as well as developing the capabilities for exploration. They are used to exploiting a mature business, hence they try to relate those processes to an innovation/entrepreneurial project ... and that is a formula for disaster. We have learnt that a project like Nexentia needs to have a dedicated and highly committed team, and that they need to think and act as entrepreneurs, not as employees exploiting a mature business. This has led us to work hard, especially on our culture, on new processes, on new methodologies, and [to] reengineer variable compensation specially drafted to a team like Nexentia.

Second, this project comes about from open innovation, from technologies developed at a research group in a public university with a totally different culture than ours. Hence, not only did we have to develop capabilities of negotiating intellectual property and technology transfer, we also had to learn to work efficiently with a research group outside our organization, mainly through building trust.

As a family member, it is more interesting to do something with higher risk. There are many tensions: shorter term results are expected; Nexentia is backed by Corona's CEO. But, people in general in the company say "it's been five years." They are short term oriented, but we are long term in Nexentia. A few days ago, one of the people in budgeting, said, "because of Nexentia, the EBITDA (earnings before interest, taxes, depreciation and amortization) of other companies is being affected, which affects our variable compensation.' Nexentia is recognized, but when they rely on variable compensation, it is an expense, and people begin to realize it is affecting them.

Innovation as a Source of Valuing Family Diversity
I was in the Family Council, where I realized that our model needed to shift so that family members could be more than a source of conflict, but also a source of value. We changed the protocol from [a] maximum two-year internship for family members to five years working in the business. Family conversations are changing. The system has to change, with opportunities for career with the company, unlike the past fifty years where due to Colombia's political problems, we grew up in New York, Miami, and Europe. This, in turn, has created a gap between the family and the business. Will the family continue to see Corona as something we have temporarily inherited and needs nurturing to pass on to next generation? Or will the family see Corona as just another investment?[28]

Additional conclusions from Corona and Nexentia. What further organizational lessons for supporting entrepreneurial behavior can we draw from the experiences of Corona and the Echavarría family? There was an entrepreneurial and opportunity mind-set from the beginning, with the founder bringing his children into the business. As circumstances became less favorable for the original import business, finding a local business that no one else thought attractive and figuring out a way to make it profitable provided another opportunity to be entrepreneurial and develop capabilities.

- *Continuous innovation utilizing application of technology and new applications of component materials.* Moving from mining into manufacturing ceramics, into sanitary ware and tiles, then into retailing, was one large and long stream, constantly building on logical extensions of unfolding opportunities, and learning to extract components of what was mined and sell those for other uses, which also led to profitable diversification.

- *Multiple partnerships.* The company took advantage of partners both to utilize knowledge they didn't have and also to spread financial risk. When attempting open, breakthrough innovation it was able to partner with a research university with a much more flexible, open culture and learn from that.

- *Recognition of the need for ambidexterity with a separate internal spinoff.* Although there had been considerable innovation in the organization's history, driven by a next-generation family member in recognition of increased competition, there was a desire to greatly accelerate the possibility of innovation for massive growth. A separate organization would be necessary because this venture would require greater risk and experimentation, with many unknowns and much more uncertainty about outcomes and therefore a need for different time horizons and skills. It was kept within the overall family group, however, probably because there had previously been diverse units, and the desire was to benefit from the strength of the total organization. The differences in required behavior turned out to be even greater than anticipated; driving core business has much shorter time horizons and less patience for experimentation and failure. It is one thing to talk about trying for breakthrough innovation, and quite another to actually pursue it within the overall business.

- *Risk was bounded by being contained within the overall organizational research and development budget.* When there was no certainty that the experiments would work, spending was limited.

As there began to be some success, however, new decisions had to be made about higher spending levels.

- *Increased spending began to encounter resistance from ongoing parts of the organization.* There is no perfect organizational structure. A completely separate structure for radical innovation would have more freedom but higher risk and less support from the parent organization. If it is incorporated within the organization (as Nexentia was within Corona), resentment can begin to arise from those with shorter-term horizons. The family will have to sort out its objectives and balance these considerations. Managing for current success and entrepreneurial growth across generations still requires balance and wisdom, not simple formulas. It requires family collaboration.

- *Innovation and changing external conditions are causing need for changes in family rules and structures.* Family members are becoming a source of value, not just of conflict. But this requires new structures and rules for participation.

Sustaining innovation is never easy, and the more that an innovation differs from existing ways of doing things—products, markets, techniques, processes, required skills, and so on, the greater will be the need for mastering ambidexterity. Organizational mechanisms that encourage entrepreneurial initiative, like those at Menasha that led a group of managers to create a successful retail packaging initiative without asking permission from above, are an important way to keep innovation coming across generations. But it also takes the individual courage of an Alexis Sabet Echavarría to push for and keep pushing on his family organization to create a sufficiently separate but connected organizational unit for breakthrough innovation, to try to help institutionalize a mechanism for future generations. Organizations shape people and people shape organizations. It is a never-ending process of experimentation and learning, which in itself is at the heart of entrepreneurial practice.

WORK SHEET 6

Reflect on the following questions to see how your enterprise is currently designed to create incremental, progressive, and radical innovations, and consider the steps that may help to enhance the chances of long-term entrepreneurial success across generations.

Areas to Consider	Yes or No If No, Useful to Initiate?	Steps to Take, Including Assignment of Responsibility for Implementation
Is your enterprise prepared for ongoing entrepreneurial behavior?		
Does your corporate governance structure have a mix of family and nonfamily members?		
Does your corporate governance structure have a mix of backgrounds and areas of expertise?		

Is your corporate governance structure open to evaluation and appropriate turnover of members?		
Is there an enterprise mechanism for encouraging and evaluating new ideas?		
Does the enterprise have a clear idea of the maximum it is willing to lose on unproven activities?		
Does the enterprise climate encourage sensible risk and not punish failures? Are employees intimidated by senior managers?		
Are there opportunities for outside alliances and collaboration to increase learning?		
Are new proposals evaluated differently from ongoing possibilities, recognizing the greater uncertainty for new activities?		
For new activities, does the organization devise quick action tests to check assumptions?		

Does the company keep its focus on efficiency in the core business(es) even while encouraging innovation and experimentation?		
• Available forum(s) for discussing innovative incremental, progressive and breakthrough ideas? If not, how can we create them? • Do we need to work on creating more, or less, risk? • Are we tapping the talents and ideas of all generations of family members, to the best of their capacities? Are they getting fullest exposure to broadening experiences? What can we do to ensure fresh ideas coming into the family and business? • Are we tapping the talents and ideas of nonfamily members? How do we get them engaged and committed? • Are we comfortable with the idea of balance among differing and apparently opposite elements of managing?		

Chapter 7.

ACTION PLANNING, A QUESTION OF BALANCE & TIMING

E nterprising families nurture the entrepreneurial spirit in every generation. The potency and challenge, charm and terror of their context is that both families and businesses are infinitely intricate systems. When mixed together, they provide a multilayered tapestry of possibilities. As the examples in this book show, there are multiple options for action. The question is *what to do, when? When should the target for change be at the organizational, familial, or personal level?* The least complex first step is to focus on the personal level and prepare a learning and entrepreneurial leadership skill development plan for yourself. It generally helps to discuss and refine the plan with family members who can facilitate it. A focus on continuous development makes it easier to understand different perspectives and ideas. It also helps to temper the perceptions of being "privileged" or "spoiled" that are often attributed to family members from successful enterprises. In addition, it enhances the feelings of excitement and humility that are an inevitable part of the learning mode. Perhaps best of all, openness to learning is contagious and encourages other family members to undertake new developmental activities too.

Enterprising families manage for the long run.[1] Their focus is not, per se, to protect the firm that the founding generation might have established. Rather it is to maintain the entrepreneurial spirit of the founders and regenerate the enterprise several times during the life span of each subsequent generation. As a steward of the family enterprise, each generation builds on the work of previous generations while preparing the next generation of entrepreneurial leaders. To endure over time, both the family and the business system must be functional. In his classic 1987 book *Keeping the Family Business Healthy,* John Ward observes that in making decisions, some families tend to pay more attention to the needs of the family system, while others focus more on the needs of the business. He referred to these as the "family first" and the "business first" philosophies. The relative focus on one dimension leads to stronger performance in that dimension, often at the cost of the other. That is, either the family functions well, or the business prospers. Only a small proportion of families in business achieve a successful balance between building strong family connections *and* making decisions that lead to strong financial performance.[2] In other words, they aim for "warm hearts *and* deep pockets" (table 7a). Maintaining this ambidexterity over time requires wisdom, courage, and patience. Both the family and the business must have inbuilt renewal mechanisms so each can regenerate to remain in harmony with the changes in internal context and external environment. But, *what to attend to when* is a question of balance and timing—a perpetual dilemma that enterprising families face in their long journey to develop entrepreneurs in every generation.

A functional family that is cohesive and adaptable is necessary for enduring business success. Firms with deep pockets but tension-prone or failed family relationships—"pained hearts"—can last for some time but usually are not sustainable. Firms with "warm hearts but empty pockets" that have a struggling business can also endure for a fairly long period of time, as the close family relationships serve as a kind of glue. Family members tighten their expenses and work harder for longer hours and less returns to make ends meet. But the accumulated depletion of financial resources eventually causes stress in the family relationships as well. Finally, firms with neither warm hearts nor deep pockets do not last very long, though they may serve as a learning ground that lets some family members start other businesses. Which of the four cells in the next table best represents your current situation?

	Level of Success on the Family Dimension	
	High	Low
High	*Warm Hearts, Deep Pockets* High Emotional and Financial Capital Can sustain successful family enterprises across generations	*Pained Hearts, Deep Pockets* High Financial but Low Emotional Capital Can last for some time but usually does not turn out to be sustainable
Low	*Warm Hearts, Empty Pockets* High Emotional but Low Financial Capital Can endure fairly long because the close family relationships serve as glue, but the accumulated depletion of the financial resources begins to stress the family relationship as well	*Pained Hearts, Empty Pockets* Low Financial and Emotional Capital Does not last very long, though may serve as a learning ground that launches some family members into starting other businesses

(Left side, rotated: Level of Success on Business Dimension)

Table 7a: Family and/or Business Success[3]

When to Address the Family System First

At times it can be hard to distinguish between family and business challenges since they often are or appear to be inextricably intertwined. If a family is unsure of the degree of alignment in its goals or beliefs and has difficulty communicating openly, that situation needs to be addressed first. Functional[4] families can openly discuss issues and ideas with each other, and the members have freedom to make independent decisions without causing resentment or hurting relationships. They are described as "close but not enmeshed." They are also adaptable and cope more effectively with changes that life presents.[5] One global assessment of the family functioning in everyday tasks across domains is the APGAR scale, which measures the following five dimensions:

- **A**daptation is the use of intra- and extra-familial resources for problem solving when family equilibrium is stressed during a crisis.

- **P**artnership is the sharing of decision making and nurturing responsibilities by family members.

- **G**rowth is the physical and emotional maturity and self-fulfillment that family members achieve through mutual support and guidance.

- **A**ffection is the caring, loving relationships that exists among family members.

- **R**esolve is the commitment to devote time to other members of the family for physical and emotional nurturing. It also usually involves a decision to share wealth and space.

Following are several statements about you and your business family. Please indicate how often you are satisfied with that aspect of your family life. Add the numbers to get your score and check the endnote for its interpretation.[6]

You are satisfied	Never	Hardly ever	Some of the time	Almost always	Always
... that you can rely or depend on your family for help when something is troubling you.	1	2	3	4	5
... with the way your family discusses things with you and shares problems with you.	1	2	3	4	5
... that your family accepts and supports your wishes to take on new activities or directions.	1	2	3	4	5
... with the way your family expresses affection and responds to your emotions, such as anger, sorrow, or love.	1	2	3	4	5
... with the way your family and you spend time together.	1	2	3	4	5

Table 7b: The APGAR Scale of Family Functioning[7]

Strengthening Family Functionality

Almost every family has its taboo subjects. It can be hard to get tough issues on the table in a productive way. Without skilled professional help, the emotional work needed to address the issues of a currently dysfunctional family probably won't be successful. But families determined to succeed over generations meet this challenge head-on. They understand that in the natural course of a business's development, at times the business system receives more attention at the cost of the family. Even when they are in contexts where the idea of seeing a family business advisor is new or underappreciated, those determined to succeed over generations educate themselves through organizations like the Family Firm Institute or networks of family business owners in their region to identify resources who can help. If they have identified the issue and understand the harm being done, savvy individuals may encourage family members to attend an educational program or visit other enterprising families that may have gone through similar experiences. Another option is to seed ideas by distributing family business–focused magazines like *Family Business* or *Tharawat* or articles and books on relevant topics. Often multiple family members enroll together in family business–focused educational programs and conferences to learn from hearing others' experiences. Through such learning, they realize that if a family is willing to consult with a tax lawyer, or a spiritual adviser, or a medical doctor, or insurance expert, or any other expert, it might also be prudent to engage experienced experts to rebuild or strengthen family functionality. In turn, such strength can help build and sustain the enterprise over time. It is useful to remember that even great athletes at the top of their games have coaches and practice daily. Isn't the family health at least as important?

Even if functionality is not a concern, there are other areas for the family to work out if they are unclear. These are usually less problematic and therefore less urgent to resolve, though necessary for long-term success. Like many problems in life, however, they are easier to resolve if addressed early, before tensions arise and participants become emotional and invested. Often families avoid such issues until disputes begin to cause strong feelings. These might be tackled when connected business issues make them salient, though it is better to address them beforehand.

But even in reasonably functional business families conflicts arise in the natural course of life. The subject of differences and influence runs just below the surface. Our conversations with family members are filled with influence questions of all kinds that echo many of the topics in this book. Here is a small sampling of the issues enterprising family members say they want to resolve:

"My kids go off and get educated, then say that they don't want to come back into our perfectly good and prosperous family business."

"One of my kids has total wanderlust and doesn't want to settle down."

"I've got two kids who insist on studying the wrong subjects; don't they know that engineering or business is what will really help us?"

"My son is a manager in the business but is just too soft with employees."

"My daughter is very ambitious, but she thinks that she has to bring the hammer down on everyone in order to prove herself."

"My father is so set in his ways that he's against anything I want to try; I learned a lot at business school that would really help us."

"My father says that his grandfather, the founder, would never have done it that way so we won't either."

"My parents won't take any risk at all."

"My cousin thinks he can manipulate his way into running the company, but I've read Machiavelli too!"

"My older brother thinks he is entitled to run things, but I understand the business a lot better than he does and I'm smarter anyway."

All of these are common influence challenges. There are innumerable others, and the following set of propositions will aid any family members wishing to address such challenges.

Iron Laws of Influence for Enterprising Families[8]

- *Reciprocity is universal.*

- *Influence is built out of reciprocity and exchange.* People allow themselves to be influenced because they believe that in some way, sooner or later, they will be "paid back" with something they value. In families, that which is valued may be love or emotional support, and the temporal span may be across generations.

- *Respect all stakeholders.* Honor them even when you cannot understand or disagree with their way of doing things. Despite your different ideas, don't present them as proving the other family member wrong. Understand the "why" behind the disagreement, as therein lies the seed to entrepreneurial ideas.

- *Start with what's in it for those you wish to influence.* For example: Preserving the future of the company? Keeping the family together? Honoring family values (especially going back to the values of the founders in their early days)? Preserving their dignity? Recognizing their contributions over the years? Minimizing risks to the family fortune? Contributions to the community or country? Better servicing customers? Preserving political connections? Try to link these (or other interests) to what you engage about or offer (preferably before you ask for anything).

- *Treat every new goal as an experiment or pilot project.* Create data, learn from it, and adjust as you go. Let others help.

- *Emphasize the opportunity for you to learn, rather than how this will prove others should have learned.* Learn from opponents too; they often see important things to take into account, and don't give them another reason to be irritated because you ignored them.

- *Provide service to the business or family that no one else wants to do, in order to build credibility and earn "credits" for later exchange.*

- *Outwork everyone, even if it is sometimes at things that you would rather not be doing.* It will be noticed.

- *See if you can find ways to expose other members (and yourself) to what is going on in other similar and different companies and industries.* Look for interesting conferences you can jointly attend. See if it is possible to jointly visit a company they respect.

- *Look for influential allies.* Board members? Company consultants? Senior family advisors? Family friends with appropriate experiences? Government officials/agencies looking to promote particular kinds of change? Whoever they are, get to know them, find common grounds, cultivate the relationships, ask for their help once you understand their common interests. Always be looking for what you can do for them.

- *Be thoughtful, kind, and generous to even the lowest-level people in the company.* Not only will your kindness always be appreciated and repaid, but it is worthwhile in its own right. And you never know what others know that they can choose to tell you if they feel you are worthy.

- *Enterprising families value the "we" over the "I."* They prefer going together slowly and far, rather than going fast alone.

The challenges and dilemmas of enterprising families can manifest themselves in several forms when it comes to balancing current operations and future possibilities. For example, which family members should be involved in the management, ownership, or governance of the family enterprise? More often than not, enterprising families have a portfolio of operations that need attention. What qualities are and will be needed in each operation, both as it exists today and might exist in the future? Family members vary in their interests and capabilities. It makes sense to bring the family together to examine just what resources exist now and are likely to develop. How many members are there in the extended family? How many are already in the family businesses? How many have expressed an interest? How many have training that is either directly relevant (such as technical, business, legal, or communications) or more general (such as history, philosophy, literature, or science)? Have some family members traveled extensively or even lived in other countries? Do some seem particularly skilled at dealing with people or at interacting with those who are different from them? Are there any family members who will need special medical, educational, or emotional support?

When should the target for change be at the organizational, familial, or personal level?

Another set of dilemmas relates to business income. How much should be distributed to (family) shareholders as opposed to reinvested in the business. How much, if any, should be borrowed for reinvestment? How much should be set aside for a risky possible breakthrough innovation as opposed to minor incremental innovation? This obviously can have a large impact on future entrepreneurial innovation. And willingness to set aside money for investment can change as the family life cycle and the composition of family members change. This kind of analysis can be most helpful when paired with an analysis of the business environment and the likely needs of the family enterprise. Indeed, most innovations in family businesses arise from small off-shoots of current operations, what could be called "strategic scraps."[9] These were filed away or sidelined because they were not core at the time somebody noticed or because there weren't sufficient resources to pursue them at the time. Enterprising families like those running Curtis Packaging, Falck Group, Brown Brothers, Lamborghini, and Supreme Creations all found the seeds of their next radical innovation from within their current business. Awareness of possible innovations can come from paying attention to what family members know from their background and experiences, as well as what they might know from the operations of the business.

Many variations are possible and can be workable, though any will have limitations, often unanticipated. If many family members and several generations are involved, any change will require a formal structure for participation and a clear decision-making process, not just informal discussions. Will the very idea of widespread family involvement be welcomed or resisted? If it will be welcomed, it must still be organized so everyone feels that it is under control and moving forward reasonably. The larger challenge, however, may be to engage family members who resist the idea of opening up discussion and to influence them, over time, to see that the long-term best interest of the family requires such engagement.

Complicating these issues is the question of who gets to decide all this and set the rules! These connect to the family vision and brand, which may or may not be explicitly spelled out. Perhaps proposing some joint family work to explore its vision or brand, because it is directed to the future, can engage the family in constructive conversations that are not quite as emotional as direct arguments about immediate investment or dividend policy. However, these can set the stage for that kind of eventual decision also. That circles back to family governance and the equivalent of the family constitution or its rules for how decisions will be made.

Many families have underutilized but highly talented resources. Examples include a daughter, daughter-in-law, or mother who may have stayed at home to raise a family. After the children are grown, she might be in a good position to devote the time and energy needed to develop family rules and constitution. Other times, it may be a member of the senior generation who has passed the operational responsibility to the next generation or a family member who may be between jobs or who just sold or closed an enterprise. Any of those, if talented, could be engaged to take on project-based initiatives that help govern the enterprising family. Of course, some families prefer to bring in experienced outsiders to handle important projects aimed at setting up or amending the ground rules or to facilitate the possibly heated discussions. As with any group of people and a potentially divisive topic, discussion will occur; the question is whether it will be open and accessible or happen covertly, in small, unhappy groupings. The latter seldom produces anything good, especially in the way of cohesion or "warm hearts."

Enhancing Business System Flexibility

At the heart of engendering entrepreneurship in every generation is the need for ambidexterity between current operations and innovations for the future. If the business is doing poorly—not growing in sales, market share, profitability, return on equity, return on total assets, profit margin on sales, or the ability to fund growth from profits and to retain or attract needed employees—then there are many well-known analytical techniques for tackling these issues. These are tools taught in most business schools, including strategy, financial analysis, process analysis, marketing, market segmentation and market research, leadership and human resource management, and so on. For example, would distribution expenses be cut by using an app for making truck routing more efficient, or marketing made more effective by using Google analytics to track website keywords to improve usage results, or costs recalculated through ABC analysis to refine product lines or to close a non-performing office? If there are family members of the next generation with the necessary skills, it can be useful to give them clearly defined projects to improve one or more of the identified issues for the enterprise and to increase their self-confidence and engagement. Alternatively, numerous consulting firms do this kind of work. The challenge is to pick one that understands and has experience working with family enterprises so they will bring the right analysis and techniques to your company's particular problems and not just apply their favorite solutions, whether or not they fit the problems. Comparison shopping and due diligence are in order. There are many good firms doing family business consulting; chemistry between consultant and client matters, not just competence, so there should be no shame in honest exploration with several firms to find one where there is good fit. Families that are adept at developing entrepreneurs in every generation use such opportunities so that incumbent leaders work closely with next-generation members to identify and work with the experts.

Many families have underutilized but highly talented resources.

The greater challenge comes when a company is strong on the operational side of the business but less good at creating the innovative atmosphere that helps generate and support new ideas that can renew products, processes, markets, and talent. To address such a challenge, a long-term campaign to alter the mind-set and practices of the firm will be required. This is seldom easy, and like all internal change projects, it needs a special combination of long-term persistence and short-term patience. Achieving major change in an existing organization requires creation, articulation, and acceptance of a vision of a future that is clear and sufficiently compelling to attract and unite most decision-makers and others in the organization.[10] In addition, there must be moderate dissatisfaction with the status quo and reasonably clear tools and pathways showing how to get to the future state. Without all of these elements, even brilliant efforts to produce desperately needed change usually fail. If people don't see where they are going or its value, they won't join. If they are either quite happy with the way things are or so unhappy that they are paralyzed by fear, they won't move. And if they are highly motivated but don't have any idea of what to do, they also won't change. Finally, if too much effort is required, they may give up.[11] How does each of these components apply to your family business?

If the family has for years prided itself on growing and learning, as do most enterprising families we have described in earlier chapters, the task will be to show how the changes supporting innovation relate to the family vision and how they support existing goals and traditions. It may, however, be necessary to dig very hard for connections to unarticulated and forgotten goals of the original founders of the business, or it may be necessary to propose that the family spend time, probably off-site, exploring what they are good at, what makes them different, what they really care about, what they can build for the future, what would make the business viable and inspiring to younger family members as well as employees, and similar questions. Outside help is not required but could be useful if the family is not accustomed to thinking or talking that way. And it may take more than one meeting to work through these issues.[12]

Research confirms that family enterprises are slow at articulating a clear vision for innovation. But once there is a clear vision, the implementation is extremely efficient.[13] A mix of family and nonfamily professionals join forces to achieve the desired objectives. Sometimes family members have alternated with professionals in running the enterprise, as at Menasha, and at other times there has been a gradual movement towards nonfamily members in executive positions or on the board, as at Pantaleón. In some companies only a few family members are allowed to hold operating positions in the enterprise or even none at all, as in the Burman family group. Several organizations used alliances and partnerships to stimulate new possibilities, including Esau Oilfield Supplies, ATF, McCain Foods, and Tetra Pak. The question, of course, is what has the innovation journey of your enterprise been over the past and how is the river going to flow forward in the future? Many different tributaries can keep the innovation stream coming.

In closing, we leave you with the following quote from Jette Egelund.[14] She took over the small workshop in which her father, Holger Nielsen, made the first pedal bin—Vipp—for his wife Marie's hairdressing salon. Working closely with her son and daughter, she has developed a large range of product lines for the company, including one that is now at the Museum of Modern Art in New York.

We didn't have any money.

We just had a big dream.

We were just modest Danish people, with no private equity, no investments.

But we worked hard, and we made it.

I think anyone who runs a family business should remember this:

Don't make excuses; if you're humble, you can dream big.

And if you work hard you can actually make your dreams come true.

LIST OF COMPANIES

Company Name	Country of Origin	Date of Founding	Original industry	Section of Book
3M www.3M.com	United States	1902	Mining	Ch1
ABC Recycling www.abcrecycling.com	Canada	1912	Scrap peddling	Ch4
Alliance Building Service www.alliancebuildingservice.com	United States	2009	Commercial cleaning & maintenance	Ch2
Amarelli Liquorice www.amararelli.com	Italy	1731	Licorice	Ch4, Ch5
Ambani www.ambanicera.com	India	1989	Ceramic tiles	Intro
Ananasa.com www.ananasa.com	United Arab Emirates	2011	Middle Eastern arts and crafts	Ch1
Apollo Hospitals www.apollohospitals.com	India	1989	Hospital chain	Ch3
Apple www.apple.com	United States	1976	Apple computers	Ch1
ATF www.atf-inc.com	United States	1946	Fasteners	Ch6, Ch7
ATF-EJOT Joint Venture www.atf-inc.com	Mexico	2007	Fasteners	Ch6
Automatic Manufacturing Limited www.automatic.com.hk	Hong Kong	1976	Engineering jobs at airports	Ch4

Company Name	Country of Origin	Date of Founding	Original industry	Section of Book
Beales Hotel www.bealeshotel.co.uk/	United Kingdom	1907	Lodge	Ch1
Berkshire Hathaway / Valley Falls Company berkshirehathaway.com	United States	1839	Textile manufacturing	Ch3
Bombardier www.bombardier.com	Canada	1937	Aerospace and transportation	Ch3
Bremen Casting www.bremencastings.com	United States	1939	Machine shop	Ch1
Brown Brothers www.brownbrothers.com.au	Australia	1889	Wine	Ch2
Business Families Foundation www.businessfamily.org	Canada	1999	Family foundation	Ch4
Canon www.canon.com	Japan	1937	Camera	Ch3
Caran d'Ache www.carandache.com/en/	Switzerland	1915	Pencils	Intro, Ch1
Carlson Company www.carlson.com	United States	1914	Hospitality	Ch3
ChariCycles www.charicycles.com	United Arab Emirates	2014	Up-cycling	Ch1
Chick-fil-A www.chick-fil-a.com	United States	1946	Restaurant	Ch3

Company Name	Country of Origin	Date of Founding	Original industry	Section of Book
Coca Cola www.coca-cola.com	United States	1886	Soft drink	Ch2
Construct Co (disguised)	Spain	1960	Construction	Ch5
Conzerv now Schneider electric www.schneider-electric.com	India	1986	Energy meters	Ch6
Corning Glass Works www.corning.com	United States	1851	Glass products	Ch5
Corona www.corona.com	Colombia	1881	Textiles	Ch6
Curtis Packaging www.curtispackaging.com	United States	1845	Comb and button manufacturing	Ch5, Ch7
Dabur www.dabur.com	India	1884	Health clinic	Ch6
Delaware North www.delawarenorth.com	United States	1915	Popcorn and peanut vending	Ch2
Dorsett Hospitality www.dorsett.com	Hong Kong	2007	Hotel	Ch3
Dot Foods www.dotfoods.com	United States	1960	Food industry redistribution	Intro, Ch2
Dublin Cleaners www.dublincleaner.com	United States	1981	Dry cleaner	Ch2

Company Name	Country of Origin	Date of Founding	Original industry	Section of Book
EJOT www.ejot-usa.com	Germany	2001	Fastening technology	Ch6
Esau Oilfield Supplies Company www.esauoilfield.com	Trinidad & Tobago	1972	Oilfield supplies	Ch3, Ch6, Ch7
Ettinger www.ettinger.com.uk	United Kingdom	1934	Leather goods	Ch1, Ch3
Facebook www.facebook.com	United States	2004	Social network services	Ch2
Falck Group www.falck.com	Italy	1906	Steel	Intro, Ch7
Fernley & Fernley Inc. www.fernley.com	United States	1886	Association management company	Ch2
Fidelitone Logistics www.fidelitone.com	United States	1983	Supply chain management company	Ch3
Fidelity Investments www.fidelity.com	United States	1946	Mutual fund and financial services	Ch3
Garcia-Tuñón www.garciatunon.com	Venezuela	1963	Chevrolet Dealership	Ch6
Gekkeikan www.gekkeikan-sake.com	Japan	1637	Sake and plum wine	Ch4
Group Park Ave www.groupeparkavenue.com/en	Canada	1959	Chevrolet dealership	Ch6

Company Name	Country of Origin	Date of Founding	Original industry	Section of Book
Gucci www.gucci.com	Italy	1921	Leather goods	Intro
Hemas Group www.hemas.com	Sri Lanka	1948	Drugs	Ch6
Henriquez Group (no single website)	El Salvador	1926	Retail store	Ch2
Henry Ford www.ford.com	United States	1903	Automotive industry	Ch2
Houshi Ryokan www.ho-shi.co.jp	Japan	718	Inn	Ch3, Ch4
Illinois Consolidated Telephone Company www.consolidated.com	United States	1924	Telephones	Ch1
J.D. Power and Associates www.jdpower.com	United States	1968	Automobile quality	Ch3
Jean Roze http://www.soieries-jean-roze.com/en/	France	1650	Silk upholstery	Ch5
Johann Diederich Neuhaus www.jdngroup.com	Germany	1745	Wooden shaft winches	Ch3
Johannes Klais Orgelbau www.orgelbau-klais.com	Germany	1882	Pipe organs	Intro
Kikkoman www.kikkoman.com	Japan	1917	Soy sauce	Ch3

Company Name	Country of Origin	Date of Founding	Original industry	Section of Book
Kongo Gumi www.japanartsandcraft.com	Japan	1615	Temple construction	Ch5
KPRT (disguised)	India	1993	Infrastructure construction	Ch5
Lamborghini www.lamborghini.com	Italy	1963	Automobiles	Ch1, Ch7
Lego www.lego.com	Denmark	1932	Toy building blocks	Ch5
Louis Vuitton www.louisvuitton.com	France	1854	Designier bags	Ch3
Luck Companies www.luck.com	United States	1923	Crush stone, sand, gravel	Ch1
McCain Foods www.mccainfoods.com	Canada	1957	Frozen french fries	Intro, Ch5, Ch7
McKinsey Consulting www.mckinsey.com	United States	1926	Global management consulting company	Ch1
Menasha Corporation www.menasha.com	United States	1849	Wooden pails	Ch1, Ch3, Ch4, Ch6
Menon and Menon www.menon.in	India	1954	Diesel engines	Ch6
Michelin www.michelinman.com	France	1888	Tires	Ch5

Company Name	Country of Origin	Date of Founding	Original industry	Section of Book
MSI www.msi.com	US Virgin Islands	1970	Building supplies	Ch6
News Corp www.newscorp.com	Australia	1923	Newspaper	Ch1
Nishiyama Onsen Keiunkan www.japanican.com	Japan	705	Inn	Ch4
Otto Group www.ottogroup.com	Germany	1949	Mail-order shoes	Ch5
Pantaleón Group www.pantaleon.com	Guatemala	1849	Sugar	Ch6
Paragon Footwear www.paragonfootwear.com	India	1975	Footware	Ch6
Paris Group of Companies http://www.bayt.com/en/company/paris-group-574400/	United Arab Emirates	1985	Retail	Ch4
Pharma Co www.pharma.us.novartis.com	Spain	1960	Construction	Ch5, Ch 6
Popular Automobiles www.popularmaruti.com	India	1944	Auto spare parts	Ch6
Rita Marquez (disguised)	Latin America	1955	Pharmaceutical distribution	Ch2
Ritter www.ritterag.com	United States	1907	Cotton	Ch6

Company Name	Country of Origin	Date of Founding	Original industry	Section of Book
Rumpke Waste and Recycling www.rumpke.com	United States	1932	Trash removal	Ch2
Rupert Murdoch www.newscorp.com	Australia	1979	Multinational mass media	Ch1, Ch2
SC Johnson www.scjohnson.com	United States	1886	Flooring	Ch2, Ch3, Ch4
Scherrer Metec AG no website, business ended	Switzerland	1896	Plumbing and roofing workshop	Ch1
Steve Harvey www.steveharvey.com	United States	NA	Comedian and actor	Ch2
Subway www.subway.com	United States	1965	Sandwiches	Ch1
Supreme Creations www.supreme-creations.co.uk	United Kingdom	Early 2000s	Bags	Intro, Ch7
Suzuki www.suzuki.com	Japan	1909	Motocycles, ATVs, scooters	Ch3
Tension Corporation www.tensioncorp.com	United States	1886	Envelopes	Intro, Ch2, Ch3
Tetra Pak AB www.tetrapak.com	Sweden	1951	Food packaging	Ch5, Ch7
The Murugappa Group www.murugappa.com	India / Burma	1900	Business comglomerates	Intro, Ch1

Company Name	Country of Origin	Date of Founding	Original industry	Section of Book
Toraya www.toraya-group.co.jp	Japan	1526	Confections	Ch5
Toyota www.toyota.com	Japan	1937	Automotive manufacturer	Ch3, Ch5
U-Haul www.uhaul.com	United States	1945	Truck rentals	Ch1
Vipp www.vipp.com	Denmark	1939	Rubbing bins	Ch4, Ch7
Walmart www.walmart.com	United States	1962	International discount retailer	Intro, Ch3, Ch5
Walt Disney www.disney.com	United States	1923	Animation industry	Ch2
WJ Towell www.wjtowell.com	Oman	1866	Trading	Ch6
WL Gore www.gore.com	United States	1958	Textiles	Ch5
Y.K. Almoayyed & Sons www.almoayyed.com	Bahrain	1940	Imported Electrical goods	Ch3
Zildjian Company www.zildjian.com	Constantinople	1929	Cymbals	Ch3

NOTES

Introduction

1   Davis, P. and Stern, D. (1980). "Adaptation, Survival, and Growth of the Family Business: An Integrated Systems Perspective." *Human Relations*, 34(4): 207–24.

2   Gómez-Mejía, L. R., Haynes, K. T., Núñez-Nickel, M., Jacobson, K. J. L., and Moyano-Fuentes, J. (2007). "Socioemotional Wealth and Business Risks in Family-Controlled Firms: Evidence from Spanish Olive Oil Mills." *Administrative Science Quarterly*, 52(1): 106-37.

3   tensioncorp.com

4   The family changed its name from Berkowitz to Berkley in 1941. See Feldman (2012), "The Tension Equation," *Family Business Magazine* (Nov/Dec).

5   El Agamy, R. M. (2014). "People and Pencils: The Mission of Caran d'Ache." *Tharawat Magazine* (Feb.–April): 18–25.

6   http://murugappa.com/corporate/group_profile.htm

7   Salvato, C., Chirico, F., and Sharma, P. (2010). "A Farewell to the Business: Championing Exit and Continuity in Entrepreneurial Family Firms." *Entrepreneurial and Regional Development*, 22(3/4): 321–48. Special issue on entrepreneurial families and family firms.

8   Carnegie, A. (1962). *The Gospel of Wealth and Other Timely Essays*. Cambridge, MA: The Belknap Press of Harvard University Press.

9   Of course, with today's reality it could be parent or child of either gender.

10 Tudor, N. (2015). "The Rise of Father and Daughter Businesses." June 18, BBC News: http://www.bbc.com/news/business-33151837.

11 LaPorta, R., Lopez-de-Silanes, F., and Shleifer, A. (1999). "Corporate Ownership around the World." *Journal of Finance*, 54: 471–517.

12   Hoy, F. and Sharma, P. (2010). *Entrepreneurial Family Firms*. Upper Saddle River, NJ: Prentice Hall, 5.

13   Miller, D. and LeBreton Miller, I. (2005). *Managing for the Long Run: Lessons in Competitive Advantage from Great Family Businesses*. Boston: Harvard Business Publishing, p. 2

14   Block, J. (2010). "Family Management, Family Ownership, and Downsizing: Evidence from S&P 500." *Family Business Review*, 23(2): 109–30.

15   Stone, D. (2013). "Big Family, Big Business." *Family Business Magazine* (Nov.–Dec.).

16   Gordon, G. and Nicolson, N. (2008). *Family Wars: The Real Stories behind the Most Famous Family Business Feuds*. London: Kogan Page Limited.

17   Mount, I. (2014). "A Family Feud, Uncorked in Spain." *New York Times* (July 19): 3–12.

18   "Business in the Blood" (2014). *The Economist* (November 1): 59–63.

19   Chua, J. H., Chrisman, J. J., and Chang, E. P. C. (2004). "Are Family Firms Born or Made? An Exploratory Investigation." *Family Business Review*, 17(1): 37–54.

20   Seibert, S. E and Zhou, H. (2006). "The Big Five Personality Dimensions and Entrepreneurial Status: A Meta-Analytical Review." *Journal of Applied Psychology*, 91(2): 259–71.

Chapter 1

1   Example from *Built to Last* by Collins and Porras (2002), Harper Business Essentials.

2   http://solutions.3m.com/wps/portal/3M/en_US/3M-Company/Information/Resources/History/?PC_Z7_RJH9U52300V200IP896S2Q3223000000_assetId=1319210372704

3   Kiefer, C. F. and Schlesinger, L. A. (2010). *Action Trumps Everything: Creating What You Want in an Uncertain World*. Carlton, Victoria, Australia: Black Ink Publishing.

4   Shane, S. A. (2008). *Illusions of Entrepreneurship: The Costly Myths That Entrepreneurs, Investors, and Policy Makers Live By*. New Haven, CT: Yale University Press.

5   Stewart, A. and Hitt, M. (2012). "Why Can't a Family Business Be More Like a Nonfamily Business: Modes of Professionalization in Family Firms. *Family Business Review*, 25(1): 58–86.

6   For examples, see the *Transgenerational Entrepreneurship* books based on the findings in the Successful Transgenerational Entrepreneurship Practices (STEP) project, published by Edward Elgar Publishers.

7   Rosing, K., Frese, M., and Bausch, A. (2011). "Explaining the Heterogeneity of the Leadership-Innovation Relationship: Ambidextrous Leadership." *The Leadership Quarterly*, 22(5): 956–74.

8   O'Reilly, C. A. and Tushman, M. (2013). "Organizational Ambidexterity: Past, Present and Future." *Academy of Management Perspectives*, 27(4): 324–38.

9   March, J. G. (1991). "Exploration and Exploitation in Organizational Learning." *Organization Science*, 2(1): 71–87.

10   Shotter, J. and Tsoukas, H. (2014). "In Search of Phronesis: Leadership and the Art of Judgment." *Academy of Management Learning & Education*, 13(2): 224–43.

11   http://encyclopedia.jrank.org/articles/pages/6179/DeLuca-Fred. html">DeLuca, Fred - Overview, Personal Life, Career Details, Chronology: Fred DeLuca, Social and Economic Impact

12   El Agamy, R. M. (2015). "Tonino Lamborghini: The Mechanics of Life." *Tharawat* (June 21). http://www.tharawat-magazine.com/ interviews/2145-short-film-tonino-lamborghini-the-mechanics-of-life. html?ct=t%28Newsletter_1_to_Newsletter6_23_2015%29

13   March, J. G. (1991). "Exploration and Exploitation in Organizational Learning." *Organization Science*, 2(10): 71–87.

14   Schuman, A., Stutz, S., and Ward, J. L. (2010). *Family Business as Paradox*. Houndsmills, Basingstroke, UK: Palgrave Macmillan.

     Another interesting reading on this subject from two renowned Australian scholars: Moores, K. and Barrett, M. (2010). *Learning Family Business: Paradoxes and Pathways*. Queensland, Australia: Bond University Press.

15   El Agamy, R. M. (2015). "Tonino Lamborghini: The Mechanics of Life." *Tharawat* (June 21). http://www.tharawat-magazine.com/ interviews/2145-short-film-tonino-lamborghini-the-mechanics-of-life. html?ct=t%28Newsletter_1_to_Newsletter6_23_2015%29.

16   El Agamy, R. M. (2014). "People and Pencils: The Mission of Caran d'Ache." *Tharawat* (Feb.–April): 18–25.

17   Sharma, P. and Irving, G. (2005). "Four Bases of Family Business Successor Commitment: Antecedents and Consequences." *Entrepreneurship Theory and Practice*, 29(1): 13–33.

     Dawson, A., Irving, P. G., Sharma, P., Chirico, F., and Marcus, J. (2014). "Examining the Behavioral Outcomes of Family Business Successor Commitment." *European Journal of Organizational Behavior*, 23(4): 570–81.

18   http://www.ted.com/talks/chimamanda_adichie_the_danger_of_a_single_ story

19   Boaz, N. and Fox, E. A. (2014). "Change Leader, Change Thyself." *McKinsey Quarterly* (March).

20   Shepard, S. (2013). "Generation to Generation Innovation at Menasha Corporation." *Family Business Magazine* (March–April).

21   Ananasa.com. "Made in the Middle East: The Story of the Kana'an Sisters." *Tharawat Magazine*. http://www.tharawat-magazine.com/en/family-business- issue-16/1770-ananasa-com-made-in-the-middle-east-2.

22   El Agamy, R. M. (2014). "The Luck Companies and the Value Based Leadership Journey: Interview with Three Generations of a Family Business." *Tharawat Magazine* (May–July): 18–23.

23   Mehta, P. K. and Shenoy, S. (2011). *Infinite Vision*. San Francisco: Berrett-Koehler.

24   Sarasvathy, S. (2008). "What Makes Entrepreneurs Entrepreneurial?" *Social Science Research Network*. http://papers.ssrn.com/sol3/papers.cfm?abstract_id=909038.

25   De Massis, A., Cruz, A. D., Jackson, J., Kotlar, J., and Mazzelli, A. (2014). "Beales Hotels: Embracing Change While Minding Their Own Business for Over 200 Years." *Global STEP Booklet II: Sustaining Entrepreneurial Family Businesses: Developing the Core, Expanding the Boundaries*. Eds. Sharma, P., Yusof, M., Parada, M. J., Dewitt, R. L., and Auletta, N. Babson Park, MA: Babson College.

26   Lansberg, I. (1999). *Succeeding Generations: Realizing the Dream of Families in Business*. Boston: Harvard Business Publishing, 75.

27   El Agamy, R. (2014). "Ettinger—A Lifetime Dedicated to Craftsmanship: Interview with Robert Ettinger, CEO Ettinger, United Kingdom." *Tharawat*, 22 (May/July): 28–33.

28   Grant, A. (2013). *Give and Take: Why Helping Others Drives Our Success*. Chapter 4. New York: Penguin Books.

29   Kanter, R. M. (1977, revised 1993). *Men and Women of the Corporation*. New York: Basic Books.

30   http://www.charicycles.com/about-us/

31   Ananasa.com. "Made in the Middle East: The Story of the Kana'an sisters." *Tharawat Magazine*. http://www.tharawat-magazine.com/en/family-business-issue-16/1770-ananasa-com-made-in-the-middle-east-2

32   Sullivan, F. J. (1997). *Born to Rebel: Birth Order, Family Dynamics, and Creative Lives*. New York: Vintage Books.

33   Vickers, G. (1983). *The Art of Judgment*. London: Harper & Row.

34   Cohen, A. R. and Bradford, D. L. (2010). *Influence without Authority* (2nd ed.). Hoboken, NJ: John Wiley & Sons.

     Cohen, A. R. and Bradford, D. L. (2013). *Influencing Up*. Hoboken, NJ: John Wiley & Sons.

35   Costa, S. S. (1996). "Smart Growth." *Family Business Magazine* (Summer).

36   Salvato, C., Minichilli, A. and Picarreta, R. (2012). "Faster Route to the CEO Suite: Nepotism or Managerial Proficiency. *Family Business Review*, 25(2): 206–24.

37   Green, M. (2011). *Inside the Multi-Generational Business: Nine Symptoms of Multi-Generational Stack-up and How to Cure Them*. New York: Palgrave Macmillan.

38 Steen, M. (2014). "Cast-Iron Commitment." *Family Business Magazine* (May/June).

39 Goldsmith, M. (2011). *What Got You Here, Won't Get You There: How Successful People Become Even More Successful*. Mundelein, IL: Round Table Press.

40 Costa, S. S. (1996). "Smart Growth." *Family Business Magazine* (Summer).

41 El Agamy, R. (2014). "Scherrer Moving On: Interview with Beat Scherrer, Scherrer Metec AG, Switzerland." *Tharawat*. http://www.tharawat-magazine.com/work-life-integration/2204-scherrer-moving-on.html.

Chapter 2

1 *The Edison and Ford Quote Book* (2004). Fort Myers, FL: Edison and Ford Winter Estates.

2 Davis, J. H., Schoorman, F. D., and Donaldson, L. (1997). "Toward a Stewardship Theory of Management." *Academy of Management Review*, 22(1): 20–47.

3 Shepherd, S. (2013). "Generation to Generation Innovation at Menasha Corporation." *Family Business Magazine* (March–April).

4 Barbera, F., Bernhard, F., Nacht, J., and McCann, G. (2015). "The Relevance of a Whole-Person Learning Approach to Family Business Education: Concepts, Evidence, and Implications." *Academy of Management Learning & Education*, 14(3): 322–46.

5 For an elaboration see: Le Breton-Miller, I. and Miller, D. (2015). "Learning Stewardship in Family Firms: For Family, By Family, Across the Life Cycle." *Academy of Management Learning & Education*, 14(3): 386–99.

6 Stone, D. (2013). "Big Family, Big Business." *Family Business Magazine* (Nov./Dec.).

7 Pennebaker, J. (1997). *Opening up: The Healing Power of Expressing Emotions*. New York: Guildford Press. Also, see Grant, A. (2013). *Give and Take: Why Helping Others Drives Our Success*. New York: Penguin Books.

8 Christie, J. (2013). "Interview: Margaret Atwood on Her Novel MaddAdam." *The Scotsman* (August 31).

9 Kammerlander, N., Dessi, C., Bird, M., Floris, M. and Murru, A. (2015). "The Impact of Shared Stories on Family Firm Innovation: A Multicase Study." *Family Business Review*, 28(4): 332–54.

10 http://www.scjohnson.com/en/family/johnsons.aspx

11 Cuddy, A. *Your Body Language Shapes Who You Are*. https://www.youtube.com/watch?v=Ks-_Mh1QhMc.

    Pennebaker, J. *The Secret Life of Pronouns*. https://www.youtube.com/watch?v=PGsQwAu3PzU.

12 Conant, D. R. and Norgaard, M. (2011). *TouchPoints: Creating Powerful Leadership Connections in the Smallest of Moments*. San Francisco: Jossey-Bass: A Wiley Imprint.

13　Schein, E. H. (2013). *Humble Inquiry: The Gentle Art of Asking Instead of Telling*. San Francisco: Berrett-Koehler Publishers Inc.

14　Wright, C. (2013). "The Hemi Q&A: Charlie Rose." *United Hemispheres* (January 1).

15　Schein, E. H. (2013). *Humble Inquiry: The Gentle Art of Asking Instead of Telling*. San Francisco: Berrett-Koehler Publishers Inc., 39–51.

16　Whetten, D. (1989). "What Constitutes a Theoretical Contribution?" *Academy of Management Review*, 14(4): 490–95.

17　Snell, S. M. (2015). "Son Brings Tech Skills to Dry Cleaners." *Family Business Magazine* (Jan.–Feb.): 72.

18　Miller, D., Steier, L., and Le-Breton Miller, I. (2003). "Lost in Time: Intergenerational Succession, Change, and Failure in Family Business." *Journal of Business Venturing*, 18(4): 513–31.

19　El Agamy, R. M. (2014). "A Legacy of Love: The Wonderful Story of the Henriquez Family." *Tharawat Magazine*.

20　Harvey, S. (2014). *Act Like a Success, Think Like a Success: Discovering Your Gift and the Way to Life's Riches*. New York: Amistad, Harper Collins Publishers, 4–5.

21　http://fortune.com/2014/04/10/the-fortune-interview-rupert-murdoch/

22　http://www.values.com/inspirational-quotes/6592-around-here-we-dont-look-backwards-for-very

23　http://www.forbes.com/sites/erikaandersen/2013/01/10/10-quotes-from-the-first-lady-of-the-world/#923390157f7d

24　The Case for Curiosity: Mario Livio at TEDxMidAtlantic 2012

25　http://www.businessinsider.com/book-recommendations-from-top-ceos-2015-10

26　Nonaka, I. and Takeuchi. H. (2011). "The Wise Leader." *Harvard Business Review*, 89(5).

27　Spector, B. (2015). "Young Family Member Shared Her Viewpoint on Family and Business." *Family Business Magazine* (Jan./Feb.): 8.

28　Stone, D. (2013). "Big Family, Big Business." *Family Business Magazine* (Nov./Dec.).

29　Feldman, K.L. (2012). "The Tension Equation." *Family Business Magazine* (Nov/Dec.). http://familybusinessmagazine.com/index.php?/articles/single/the_tensio.

30　Fernley, K. (2014). "Fernley & Fernley Inc." *Family Business Magazine* (Sept./Oct.): 87.

31　Donelson, D. (2015). "Emphasis on Team Work." *Family Business Magazine* (Jan./Feb.): 42–47.

32   Fairlie, R. W. and Robb, A. (2007). "Families, Human Capital, and Small Business: Evidence from the Characteristics of Business Owners Survey." *Industrial and Labor Relations Review*, 60(2): 225–45.

33   Shefsky, L. E. (2014). *Invent, Reinvent, Thrive: The Keys to Success for Any Start-up, Entrepreneur, or Family Business*. New York: McGraw Hill.

   Also see: Schlesinger, L. A., Kiefer, C. F. and Brown, P. B. (2012). *Just Start: Take Action, Embrace Uncertainty, and Create the Future*. Boston: Harvard Business Publishing.

34   Sarasvathy, S. (2001). "What Makes Entrepreneurs Entrepreneurial?" http://www.effectuation.org/sites/default/files/documents/what-makes-entrepreneurs-entrepreneurial-sarasvathy.pdf.

35   http://www.brownbrothers.com.au/about-us/our-family/

36   Disguised name.

Chapter 3

1   Created in 1981, the Henokiens is an association of companies that meet these four criterion: (i) been in existence for over 200 years; (ii) the family must be owner or majority shareholder of the company; (iii) one member of the founding family must still manage the company or be a member of the board; and (iv) the company must be in good financial health and up-to-date.

2   Sharma, P. and Salvato, C. (2013). "Family Firm Longevity: A Balancing Act between Continuity and Change." In *The Endurance of Family Business: A Global Overview*. Eds. Fernández Pérez, P. and Colli, A., 34–56. New York: Cambridge University Press.

3   McGoldrick, M., Carter, B. and Garcia-Preto, N. (2011). *The Expanded Family Life Cycle: Individual, Family, and Community Perspectives*, 4th ed. New York: Pearson.

4   Becker, Gary S. (1991). *A Treatise on the Family*. Boston: Harvard University Press.

5   Markson, E. W. (2007). *Social Gerontology Today*: An Introduction. Cary, NC: Oxford University Press.

6   Green, M. (2011). *Inside the Multi-Generational Business: Nine Symptoms of Multi-Generational Stack-Up and How to Cure Them*. New York: Palgrave Macmillan.

7   Sharma, P., Chrisman, J., and Chua, J. (2003a). "Predictors of Satisfaction with the Succession Process in Family Firms." *Journal of Business Venturing*, 18: 667–87.

8   Hoy, F. and Sharma, P. (2010). *Entrepreneurial Family Firms*. New York: Pearson Prentice Hall.

9   Nicholson, N. (2008). "Evolutionary Psychology and Family Business: A New Synthesis for Theory, Research and Practice." *Family Business Review*, 21(1): 103–18.

10   http://corporate.walmart.com/our-story/leadership/board-of-directors/gregory-penner/

11   Davis, J.A. (2015). "Developing Your Next CEO for the Family Business," *Working Knowledge* (November 24). Boston: Harvard Business School.

12   *Economist* (2012). "Adult Adoption in Japan: Keeping It in the Family." December 1.

      Mehrotra, V., Morch, R., Shim, J., and Wiwattanakantang, Y. (2013). "Adoptive Expectations: Rising Sons in Japanese Family Firms." *Journal of Financial Economics*, 108(3): 840–54.

      Feiler, B. (2013). *The Secrets of Happy Families.* New York: William Morrow, Harper Collins Publishers, 54.

13   http://www.tharawat-magazine.com/media-gallery/2093-the-world-s-oldest-company.html

14   Feiler, B. (2013). *The Secrets of Happy Families.* New York: William Morrow, Harper Collins Publishers, 62–63.

15   Feiler, B. (2013). *The Secrets of Happy Families.* New York: William Morrow, Harper Collins Publishers, 62–63.

16   http://www.chick-fil-a.com/Company/Highlights-Sunday

17   http://www.chick-fil-a.com/Company/Highlights-Fact-Sheets

18   Stone, D. (2010). "A Long Playing Legacy." *Family Business Magazine* (Autumn).

19   Feldman, K. L (2012). "The Tension Equation." *Family Business Magazine* (Nov./Dec.).

20   Shepard, S. (2013). "Generation to Generation Innovation at Menasha Corporation." *Family Business Magazine* (March/April).

21   Lansberg, I. (1999). *Succeeding Generations: Realizing the Dream of Families in Business.* Boston: Harvard Business Publishing.

22   Sharma, P. and Irving, G. (2005). "Four Bases of Family Business Successor Commitment: Antecedents and Consequences." *Entrepreneurship Theory & Practice* (January): 13–33.

23   Dawson, A., Irving, P. G., Sharma, P., Chirico, F., and Marcus, J. (2014). "Examining the Behavioral Outcomes of Family Business Successor Commitment." *European Journal of Organizational Behavior*, 23(4): 570–81.

24   Lansberg, I. (1999). *Succeeding Generations: Realizing the Dream of Families in Business.* Boston: Harvard Business Publishing.

25   http://www.peterbuffett.com/about/

26   http://www.washingtonpost.com/lifestyle/style/peter-buffett-shows-that-even-the-son-of-a-billionaire-can-pull-up-those-bootstraps/2014/10/09/ccee7b20-4fcd-11e4-babe-e91da079cb8a_story.html

27   König, A., Kammerlander, N., and Enders, A. (2013). "The Family Innovator's Dilemma: How Family Influence Affects the Adoption of Discontinuous Technologies by Incumbent Firms." *Academy of Management Review*, 38(3): 418–41.

28 Spector, B. (2013). "A New Era at Carlson." *Family Business Magazine* (Sept.–Oct.).

29 Zhao, H. and Seobert, S. E. (2006). "The Big Five Personality Dimensions and Entrepreneurial Status: A Meta-Analytic Review." *Journal of Applied Psychology*, 91: 259–71.

30 Spector, B. (2013). "A New Era at Carlson." *Family Business Magazine* (Sept.–Oct.).

31 Spector, B. (2013). A New Era at Carlson." *Family Business Magazine* (Sept.–Oct.).

32 El Agamy, R. M. (2014). "Ettinger, British Luxury Leader Good." *Tharawat Magazine* (May–July).

33 Also, lyrics by Sting, "If you love somebody set them free," http://www.sting.com/discography/lyrics/lyric/song/152

34 Spector, B. (2013). "A New Era at Carlson." *Family Business Magazine* (Sept.–Oct.).

35 Steen, M. (2014). "The Power Family's Second Chapter." *Family Business Magazine* (May/June).

Chapter 4

1 Davis, J. (2014). "Managing the Family Business: Survival's Secret Sauce." *Harvard Working Knowledge: The Thinking that Leads*. May 20. http://hbswk.hbs.edu/faculty/jdavis.html.

2 http://www.sumitomocorp.co.jp/english/company/about/sc_history/

3 Hatum, A. (2007). *Adaptation or Expiration in Family Firms*. Cheltanham, UK: Edgar Elgar.

4 Davis, J. (2014). "Managing the Family Business: Survival's Secret Sauce." *Harvard Working Knowledge: The Thinking that Leads*. May 20. http://hbswk.hbs.edu/faculty/jdavis.html.

5 Drucker, P. F. (1985). "The Discipline of Innovation." *Harvard Business Review* (May–June).

6 Sinek, S. (2009). Ted Talk: "How Great Leaders Inspire Action."

7 De Geus, A. (1997). "The Living Company." *Harvard Business Review* (March–April). Also, a book by the same title.

8 Feiler, B. (2013). *The Secrets of Happy Families*. New York: William Morrow, HarperCollins Publishers, 64–71.

9 Examples of sources listed are two books: *In Search of Excellence* and *Good to Great: Character Report Cards of the KIPP Charter Schools*; and *Character Strengths Identified by Martin Seligman, the Father of Positive Psychology*.

10 Feiler, B. (2013). *The Secrets of Happy Families*. New York: William Morrow, Harper Collins Publishers, 67.

11   Family Firm Institute is a not-for-profit professional association that is a good place to check in for facilitators for such exercises. Of course, referrals are always useful to have.

12   Lansberg, I. (1999). *Succeeding Generations: Realizing the Dream of Families in Business*. Boston: Harvard Business Publishing; 108–11.

13   Micelotta, E. R. and Raynard, M. (2011). "Concealing or Revealing the Family? Corporate Brand Identity Strategies in Family Firms." *Family Business Review*, 24(3): 197–216.

14   http://www.scjohnson.com/en/home.aspx

15   http://www.scjohnson.com/en/family/in-my-family.aspx

16   http://www.tharawat-magazine.com/art-the-family-business/1714-the-bin-that-is-art-%E2%80%93-how-a-family-invention-became-a-museum-piece-2.html

17   Salvato, C., Minichilli, A., and Piccarreta, R. (2012). "Faster Route to the CEO Suite: Nepotism or Management Proficiency." *Family Business Review*, 25(2): 206–24.

18   Au, K. and Cheng, J. (2011). "Hong Kong: Creating 'The New' through Portfolio Entrepreneurship." In Sieger, P., Nason, R., Sharma, P. and Zellweger, T. (2011). *The Global STEP Booklet: Evidence-Based, Practical Insights for Enterprising Families*.

19   Sandoval-Arzaga, F. and Fonseca-Paredes, M. (2011). "Mexico: How to Integrate Knowledge among Generations in a Family Business?" In Sieger, P., Nason, R., Sharma, P. and Zellweger, T. (2011). *The Global STEP Booklet: Evidence-Based, Practical Insights for Enterprising Families*.

20   Gagnè, M., Wrosch, C. and Brun de Pontet, S. (2011). "Retiring From the Family Business: The Role of Goal Adjustment Capacities." *Family Business Review*, 24(4): 292–94.

21   Barrett, M. and Moores, K., (2009). *Women in Family Business Leadership Roles: Daughters on the Stage*. Cheltenham, UK: Edward Elgar Publishing. Lansberg, I. (1999). *Succeeding Generations: Realizing the Dream of Families in Business*. Boston: Harvard Business Publishing.

22   Lansberg, I. (1999). *Succeeding Generations: Realizing the Dream of Families in Business*. Boston: Harvard Business Publishing.

23   Shepard, S. (2013). "Generation to Generation Innovation at Menasha Corporation." March/April.

24   Shepard, S. (2013). "Generation to Generation Innovation at Menasha Corporation." March/April.

25   El Agamy, R. (2013). "The Pains and Gains of Corporate Governance: Interview with Mohammed Abdul Rahim Al Fahim." *Tharawat*, 20: 20–26.

26   Stone, D. (2014). "ABC Recycling." *Family Business Magazine* (Sept.–Oct.).

27   Lansberg, I. (2000). "Are You Ready for the Journey?" *Family Business Magazine* (Winter).

Chapter 5

1   Miller, D. and LeBreton- Miller, I. (2005). *Managing for the Long Run: Lessons in Competitive Advantage from Great Family Businesses.* Boston: Harvard Business Publishing.

2   McConaughy, D. L. (2000). "Family CEOs vs. Nonfamily CEOs in the Family-Controlled firm: An Examination of the Level and Sensitivity of Pay to Performance." *Family Business Review,* 13(2): 121–31.

3   Greenberg, D. (2002). "Designing Effective Organizations." *The Portable MBA in Management, 2nd edition.* Ed. Cohen, Allan R. New York: John Wiley and Sons

4   Greiner, L.E. (1972). "Evolution and Revolution as Organizations Grow: A Company's Past Has Clues for Management that Are Critical for Future Success." *Harvard Business Review* (July–Aug.).

5   Lambrecht, J. and Lievens, J. (2008). "Pruning the Family Tree: An Unexplored Path to Family Business Continuity and Family Harmony." *Family Business Review,* 21(4): 295–313

6   König, A., Kammerlander, N., and Enders, A. (2013). "The Family Innovator's Dilemma: How Family Influence Affects the Adoption of Discontinuous Technologies by Incumbent Firms." *Academy of Management Review,* 38: 418–41.

7   Gimeno, A. and Parada, M. J. (2014). "Professionalization of the Family Business: Decision-Making Domains." In *Exploring Transgenerational Entrepreneurship: The Role of Resources and Capabilities.* Eds. Sharma, P., Sieger, P., Nason, R. S., Cristina Gonzalez, A., and Ramachandran, K. Cheltanham, UK: Edward Elgar Publishers.

8   Hutcheson, J. O. (2007). "The End of a 1400-year-old Business." *Bloomberg BusinessWeek* (April 16).

9   Sharma, P. (2014). "Evolution in Thinking about Generational Transition in Family Enterprises." *FFI Practitioner* (June 11). Previous research had found that only 30 percent of family businesses made it to the second generation, and 3 percent made it to the third generation, but it turns out that many families have multiple businesses in the first generation. Some are sold, and some go public, so not all fail in the conventional sense.

10 Hatum, A. (2007). *Adaptation or Expiration in Family Firms: Organizational Flexibility in Emerging Economies.* Cheltenham, UK: Edward Elgar Publishing Limited.

11 These organization innovation items come from our own observations, and our summary of relevant research gathered in Anderson, N., Potočnik, K., and Zhou, J. "Innovation and Creativity in Organizations: A State-of-the-Science Review, Prospective Commentary, and Guiding Framework." *Journal of Management,* 40(5): 1297–333; and Kanter, R. M. (1985). *The Change Masters: Innovations for Productivity in the American Corporation.* New York: Free Press. One of this book's authors is teaching, living, and researching

among some extreme high-tech, rapid growth US West Coast companies and has resisted the temptation to include (actual) amenities like free meals, a slide from the second floor to the lobby, employees zipping around on skateboards, and so on as necessities for encouraging innovation, although in the very competitive environment for retaining talent, they have come to seem to be basic necessities. One such example is reported in Cohen, A. R. (2015). "Box, Inc. Preserving Startup Culture in a Rapidly Growing Company," BAB 723 (April). Boston: Babson College, Harvard Business Publishing.

12   Rosing, K., Frese, M., and Bausch, A. (2011). "Explaining the Heterogeneity of the Leadership-Innovation Relationship: Ambidextrous Leadership." *The Leadership Quarterly*, 22: 956–74.

13   Zellweger, T. and Sieger, P. (2012). "Entrepreneurial Orientation in Long-Lived Family Firms." *Small Business Economics*, 38(1): 67–84.

14   Although ambidexterity is important, it gets used in many ways. O'Reilly, C. and Tushman, M. (2013). "Organizational Ambidexterity: Past, Present and Future." *Academy of Management Perspectives* 27: 324–38.

15   Terms to describe three degrees of innovation can vary, depending on the framework of the authors. The family business literature uses Radical, Progressive and Incremental; see for example, Bergfeld, M. M. H. and Weber, F.-M. (2011). "Dynasties of Innovation: Highly Performing German Family Firms and the Owners' Role for Innovation." *Int. J. Entrepreneurship and Innovation Management*, 13(1): 80–94). Others use Breakthrough or Revolutionary, Incremental (in place of Progressive), and Constant. One early example is Tushman, M. L. and O'Reilly, C.A. (1996).

16   Miller, D. and LeBreton-Miller, I. (2005). *Managing for the Long Run: Lessons in Competitive Advantage from Great Family Businesses*. Boston: Harvard Business Review Press. We highly recommend this book and especially its chapter on innovators, and we will mention several of their examples.

17   Gertner, J. (2007). "From 0 to World Domination." *NY Times*, Feb, 18, 2007. Japanese Kaizen, the system of constant improvement, has been extensively studied, but requires a true commitment to a culture of quality and innovation.

18   Extracted from the Jean Roze website in Micelotta, E. R. and Raynard, M. (2011). "Concealing or Revealing the Family? Corporate Brand Identity Strategies in Family Firms." *Family Business Review* 24(3): 197–216

19   TORAYA Business Case Study
www.henokiens.com/userfiles/file/Toraya_Case_study.pdf

20   Bergfeld, M-M. H. and Weber, F-M. (2011). "Dynasties of Innovation: Highly Performing German Family Firms and the Owners' Role for Innovation." *Int. J. Entrepreneurship and Innovation Management*, 13(1): 80–94.

21   Matijas, B. "Lego: From Bankruptcy to 'Everything Is Awesome.'" Posted on April 8, 2015, by *ffipractitioner*.

22 Miller, D. and LeBreton-Miller, I. (2005). *Managing for the Long Run: Lessons in Competitive Advantage from Great Family Businesses*. Boston: Harvard Business Review Press. We highly recommend this book and especially its chapter on innovators, and we will mention several of their examples.

23 Shefsky, L. E. (2014). *Invent, Reinvent, Thrive: The Keys to Success for Any Start-Up, Entrepreneur, or Family Business*. New York: McGraw-Hill.

24 Hammel, G. and Breen, B. (2007). "Building an Innovation Democracy," excerpted from *The Future of Management*. Boston: Harvard Business School Press.

25 Konig, A., Kammerlander, N., and Endersmid, A. (2013). "The Family Innovator's Dilemma: How Family Influence Affects the Adoption of Discontinuous Technologies by Incumbent Firms." *Academy of Management Review*, 38(3): 418–41.

26 Howorth, C., Allen, M., Brush, C., Calabrò, A., Gonzalez Couture, G.A., Chung, H.-M., Gimeno, A., Mohd Nor, L., Monteferrante, P., Neubaum, D., and Schwarz, T. (2015). "STEP Quantitative Survey Results 2015: Initial Report to the STEP Community." STEP Summit Reports and Resources. Paper 14.

27 Bergfeld, M-M. H. and Weber, F.-M. (2011).

28 Gimeno and Parada (2014).

29 Hall, A., and Nordqvist, M. (2008). "Professional Management in Extended Family Business: Toward an Extended Understanding. *Family Business Review*, 21(1): 51–69

30 DeWitt, R. L. and Gonzalez, A. C. (2014). "The Role of Experience and Socio-Emotional Wealth in Business Continuity." In Sharma, P. et al., *Exploring Transgenerational Entrepreneurship: The Role of Resources and Capabilities*. Northampton, MA: Elgar.

31 Ramachandran, K. and Bhatnagar, N. (2015). "Challenges of Collective Leadership." *Developing Next Generation Leaders for Transgenerational Entrepreneurial Family Enterprises*. Northampton, MA: Elgar.

32 Parada, M. J., Nordqvist, M., and Gimeno, A. (2010). "Institutionalizing the Family Business: The Role of Professional Associations in Fostering a Change of Values." *Family Business Review*, 23(4): 355–72.

33 Farmsworth, C. H. (1994). "Canadian Family's Feud." *NY Times* (October 30).

Chapter 6

1 Aronowitz, S., De Smet, A., and McGinty, D. (2015). "Getting Organizational Redesign Right." *McKinsey Quarterly* (3): 99–109.

2 Ibid.

3 http://www.darden.virginia.edu/faculty-research/directory/saras-d-sarasvathy/

4   Sarasvathy, S. D. (2001), "Causation and Effectuation: Toward a Theoretical Shift from Economic Inevitability to Entrepreneurial Contingency." *Academy of Management Review*, 26(2): 243–63; Sarasvathy, S. D. (2009). *Effectuation: Elements of Entrepreneurial Expertise*. Cheltenham, UK: Edward Elgar Publishing; and many co-authored articles since.

5   Schlesinger, L., and Keifer, C. (2010). *Action Trumps Everything: Creating What You Want in an Uncertain World*. Carlton, Victoria, Australia: Black Ink Press.

    Neck, H. M., Greene, P. G., and Brush, C. G. (2014). "Teaching Entrepreneurship as a Method That Requires Practice." *Teaching Entrepreneurship: A Practice-Based Approach*. Cheltenham, UK: Elgar.

6   Shefsky, Lloyd. E. (2014). *Invent, Reinvent, Thrive: The Keys to Success for Any Start-up, Entrepreneur, or Family Business*. New York: McGraw-Hill.

    McGrath, R., and MacMillan, I. (2009). *Discovery-Driven Growth: A Breakthrough Process to Reduce Risk and Seize Opportunity*. Boston: Harvard Business School Publishing.

7   Ward, J. L. (1987). *Keeping the Family Business Healthy: How to Plan for Continuing Growth, Profitability, and Family Leadership*. Marietta, GA: Family Enterprise Publishers.

    Ward, J. L. (1991). *Creating Effective Boards for Private Enterprises: Meeting the Challenges of Continuity and Competition*. Marietta, GA: Family Enterprise Publishers.

8   Gersick, K. E. and Neus, F. (2013). "Governing the Family Enterprise: Practices, Performance, and Research." In *SAGE Handbook of Family Business*. Eds. Melin, L., Nordqvist, M., and Sharma, P. London: Sage Publications.

9   Here and in several other places in the book we mention individual researchers, business schools, educational programs and consultants not to promote them over others but to acknowledge specific examples where they are known and publicly identified.

10 Ramachandran, K. "Indian Family Businesses: Their Survival beyond Three Generations." Indian School of Business, Working Paper Series.

11 Spector, B. (2013). "Policy for Nominating Qualified Directors." *Family Business* (Sept.–Oct.), 23(5): 8.

12 Gimeno, A. and Parada, M. J. "Professionalization of the Family Business: Decision-Making Domains," in *Exploring Transgenerational Entrepreneurship: The Rise of Resources and Capabilities*, eds. Sharma et al. Cheltenham, UK: Edward Elgar, 42–61.

13 Hall, A., and Nordqvist, M. (2008). "Professional Management in Extended Family Business: Toward an Extended Understanding." *Family Business Review*, 21(1): 51–69.

14 El Agamy, F., and Schreiber, C. (2014). "Middle East: Good Governance in Family Firms: Five Case Studies from the Middle East." Tharawat Family Business Forum and Pearl Initiative.

15   Auletta, N. Rodriguez, A., and Monteferrante, P. (2014). "Fine Tuning the Entrepreneurial Legacy across Generations of Garcia Tunon—A Venezuelan Company." In Sharma et al., eds., *Exploring Transgenerational Entrepreneurship: The Role of Resources and Capabilities*, STEP. Cheltenham, UK: Elgar.

16   Ickis, Pantaleón Group case.

17   Miller, D. and LeBreton-Miller, I. (2005). *Managing for the Long Run: Lessons in Competitive Advantage from Great Family Businesses*. Boston: Harvard Business Review Press. We highly recommend this book and especially its chapter on innovators, and we will mention several of their examples.

18   Cohen, A. R. and Bradford, D. L. (2012). *Influencing Up*, chapter 2. New York: John Wiley and Sons.

19   Mollie was not trained in consulting and was not planning a professional career in business, so was not concerned with retaliation, which proved to be an advantage in this situation.

20   Cohen, A. R., and Bradford, D. L. (2012). The biography referred to is Bhave, S. (2004). *Casting a Destiny: The Biography of Chandran Menon*. Trans. Dange, N. Pune, India: Ameya Books, 43–44.

21   Tushman, M. L., and Kiron, D. (2008/2010). "Hema Hattangady and Conserv(A)." Harvard Business School Case 409-022, December 2008 (revised December 2010).

22   Cohen, A. R. (2007). "Building a Business through Conflict: The Brunt Family and MSI." Video case of the Brunt Family. Babson, MA: Babson College.

23   Over fifty years ago, Allan Cohen observed a large family business where one second generation son, who was perceived to be less competent than his siblings, was sent to a distant small country as nominal head of a subsidiary, with a nonfamily "second-in-command" to "help" him run it.

24   El Agamy, R. (2014). "Conversation with Patricia Ghany, CFO of Esau Oilfields Supplies Company Limited, Trinidad." *Tharawat* (Feb.–April).

25   Ward, J. L. and Zsolnay, C. (2013). "ATF, Inc.: Enhancing Succession Transitions and New Entrepreneurial Activity across Generations." STEP Global Case Booklet.

26   http://www.australiasfirstfamiliesofwine.com.au/index.php

27   This description is based on the article "Generation to Generation Innovation at Menasha Corporation," by Sylvia Shepherd, (chair of the Smith Family Council and a fifth-generation owner of Menasha Corporation), *Family Business Magazine* (2013), and personal interviews with her by the authors of this book, July 8 and August 12, 2014.

28   The source for all of the material about Corona is Alexis Sabet Echavarría, a fourth-generation family member who is determined to lead breakthrough innovation through an internal startup, Nexentia, described in his recounting of the Corona history and the use of and need for ambidexterity for innovation. Alexis is also the cofounder of Morey, an agricultural company.

He also cofounded Fundacíon Delfina Contigo, which provided therapy with dolphins for children with emotional and/or physical disabilities. He was a family council member for six years and served as vice chairman for one year. He also served as a board member of Fundacíon Puntos De Encuentro, a philanthropic foundation. He has a BS in business administration, an MBA in family business from Coles College of Business, and a masters in strategy and innovation from the University of Oxford.

Chapter 7

1   Miller, D. and Le Breton Miller, I. (2005). *Managing for the Long Run: Lessons in Competitive Advantage from Great Family Businesses*. Boston: Harvard Business School Press.

2   Basco, R., and Pérez Rodriguez, M. J. (2009). "Studying the Family Enterprise Holistically: Evidence for Integrated Family and Business Systems. *Family Business Review*, 22(1): 82–95.

3   Sharma, P. (2004). "An Overview of the Field of Family Business Studies: Current Status and Directions for Future." *Family Business Review*, 17(1): 1–36.

4   Olson, D. H. (2000). "Circumplex Model of Marital and Family Systems." *Journal of Family Therapy* 22(2): 144–67, created in Sharma et al, 2013.

5   Michael-Tsabari and Lavee (2012). "Too Close and Too Rigid: Applying the Circumplex Model of Family Systems to First-Generation Family Firms." *Journal of Marriage and Family Therapy*, 38(1): 105–16

6   Scoring: <11 = Dysfunctional;   11–17 is Indeterminate; >17 = Clearly Functional

7   Danes, S. M. and Morgan, E. A. (2004). "Family Business Owning Couples: An EFT View into Their Unique Conflict Culture." *Contemporary Family Therapy*, 26(3): 241–60.

    Smilkstein, G. (1978). "The Family APGAR: A Proposal for a Family Function Test and Its Use by Physicians." *The Journal of Family Practice*, 6, 1231–39.

    Smilkstein, G., Ashforth, C., and Montano, D. (1982). "Validity and Reliability of the Family APGAR as a Test of Family Function." *The Journal of Family Practice*. 5(2): 303–11.

    Gudmunson, C. G. and Danes, S. M. (2013). "Family Social Capital in Family Businesses: A Stocks and Flows Investigation." *Family Relations*, 62, 399–414. DOI:10.111/fare.12017. For more discussion of each of the measures of family functional integrity and business-related tensions and how they relate to business success and the resilience capacity that family functioning can create or detract from the business, see also Danes, S. M. and Stafford, K. (2011). "Family Social Capital as Family Business Resilience Capacity," in Richard Sorenson, ed., *Family Business and Social Capital*, chapter 7. Cheltenham, UK: Edward Elgar, 79–105.

8 Based on concepts from Cohen, A. R. and Bradford, D. L. (2005). *Influence without Authority*, revised edition. New York: John Wiley & Sons, and *Influencing Up* (2012). New York: John Wiley & Sons.

9 We thank Prof. John Ward for introducing this idea and term to us.

10 Vaill, P. B. and Cohen, A. R. (2002) in *The Portable MBA in Management*, 2nd edition, edited by Cohen, A. R. New York: John Wiley & Sons.

11 Model adapted from David Gleicher, first introduced in Beckhard, R., and Harris, R. T. (1977). *Organizational Transitions: Managing Complex Change*. Reading, MA: Addison-Wesley.

12 For a description of one such process in a family-like company with a strong founder, see "Pharmco" in Bradford, D. L. and Cohen, A. R. (1998). *Power Up*. New York: John Wiley & Sons.

13 Chrisman, J. J. and Patel, P. C. (2012). "Variations in R&D Investments of Family and Non-Family Firms: Behavioral Agency and Myopic Loss Aversion Perspectives." *Academy of Management Journal*, 55: 976–97.

14 "The Bin That Is Art—How a Family Invention Became a Museum Piece." http://www.tharawat-magazine.com/art-the-family-business/1714-the-bin-that-is-art-%E2%80%93-how-a-family-invention-became-a-museum-piece-2.html.

ACKNOWLEDGMENTS

Many people have made important contributions to this book, but for the combination of family and business none could be more important than our parents and grandparents, the Cohen and Shatsky families for Allan, and the Dada, Joshi, and Sharma families for Pramodita. That is where we grew up and where we worked in the family businesses. We are deeply grateful for all that was imparted to us, intentionally and by the sheer opportunity of being there.

Many academic colleagues have contributed directly and indirectly to the ideas, findings, and examples in the book, or that shaped our thinking even though they do not appear in the final version. For Pramodita, the deepest insights about enterprising families come from her role as the editor of the premier journal in the field—*Family Business Review* (FBR), and at the annual conferences of the Family Firm Institute, the owner of FBR. In the last five years, 1,865 unique scholars based in seventy-two countries submitted their research for publication in FBR. While only twenty papers get accepted for publication in FBR each year, there is no submission that does not carry at least one new nugget from enterprising family firms.

We continue to learn from our students and colleagues at Babson College, the Kellogg School of Management, and the Grossman

School of Business at the University of Vermont. Our collaboration began through our work on the Successful Transgenerational Entrepreneurship Practices (STEP) project convened by Babson College. We have benefited from our interactions with the over 200 researchers and educators from the more than forty universities from around the world who are members of this project. The extended qualitative case histories of enterprising families from this project have been published in the five books and several practitioner booklets. Findings from this ongoing research continue to be shared in conferences and summits that bring families and researchers together to co-create knowledge on enterprising families.

Several people have been extremely generous in carefully reading earlier versions of this book and providing us thoughtful suggestions that have helped to sharpen our thinking and writing. The book is greatly improved because of their time and effort. Judy Green, President of the Family Firm Institute, provided provocative remarks that made us pause several times in our revisions. She challenged us to back our insights with examples and research findings. While we'd anticipate her next email with even more remarks, we hated having to go through the revision processes, knowing fully well that we must! Judy, *thank you!*

Ramia M. El Agamy, editor of *Tharawat Magazine*, was gracious in her remarks, challenging us in her gentle ways and suggesting several excellent case examples to illustrate how enterprising families were coping with the issues we raised. We are deeply grateful to John Ward, who remains an inspiration for family business scholars, educators, and advisors. Pramodita has cherished his encouragement and guidance throughout her career. We thank him for his thoughtful foreword for this book. Professor K. Ramachandaran, Executive Director of the Thomas Schmidheiny Centre for Family Enterprise at the Indian School of Business, read the manuscript and offered numerous examples to help elaborate conceptual points. We also are greatly appreciative for his special foreword for the Indian edition of the book.

Ken Moores of the Moores Family Enterprise in Australia; Mark Evans of the Coutts Institute in UK; John Ickis of INCAE; and Harry Strachan helped us with their input. We thank Sharon Danes,

Professor and Family Economist, University of Minnesota, for wisdom and support on family dynamics research and how to measure family functionality. Our appreciation goes out to *Family Business Magazine* for excellent coverage of family business experiences, many of which we use in this book.

Two former students, Sylvia Shepherd from Menasha Corporation and Patricia Silhy from the Grupo San Nicolas in Guatemala, provided wonderful detailed insider material from their companies, as did Alexis Sabet Echavarría from Corona in Colombia. Our gratitude to them, and to all our students over the years from whose experiences, comments, and questions we have learned about enterprising families. Amanda Rodrigues, formerly regional director of North America Campden Wealth, has been supportive in numerous ways.

Berrett-Kohler Publishers have been an excellent team to work with. We taxed their patience at times and have appreciated their continuous encouragement. Special thanks to our editor, Neal Maillet, who never gave up on us, even when we were delayed with our deliverables. Jeevan Sivasubramaniam from BK Publishers helped find and manage the review process leading us to the perspectives of Charles Ehrlich, Jeff Kulick, and Simon Blattner. Our thanks to Eiko Tsukamoto for graphics help and general cheerfulness.

Nevertheless, although it has taken the help of all these amazing people and many more, we still take full responsibility for the contents of this book. We hope you find it helpful to continue on the fascinating journey of building entrepreneurs in every generation of your enterprising family.

Name Index

SUBJECT INDEX

About the Authors

Allan R. Cohen, MBA with distinction and DBA from Harvard University Graduate School of Business Administration, has been at Babson since 1982. Professor Cohen holds the Edward A. Madden Distinguished Professorship in Global Leadership and is in residence at the San Francisco campus. He completed seven years as vice president of academic affairs and dean of faculty and recently served two years as the interim dean of the graduate school. He was awarded the college's highest honor, The Walter Carpenter Prize for distinguished service.

His career has been devoted to increasing the leadership and management skills of practicing and aspiring managers and to building innovative academic organizations. A consultant on organizational change and leadership for companies as large as GE, IBM, and

Lafarge, and as entrepreneurial as Access Technology and Menon and Menon Diesel Engines, he helped found the Indian Institute of Management in Ahmedabad. He has also lived and worked in the Philippines, England, and Holland and has consulted in China, Brazil, Venezuela, Ireland, Switzerland, Germany, Austria, Singapore, and Dubai. At the University of New Hampshire, he was the J. R. Carter Professor of Management and helped build the Whittemore School of Business and Economics. Throughout his career he has directed and taught in executive development programs for thousands of managers.

Dr. Cohen's first book, based on his doctoral dissertation, was *Tradition, Change and Conflict in Indian Family Business*, published by Mouton in The Hague. He is the coauthor with David Bradford of numerous books widely used by managers: the best seller *Managing for Excellence*; the award-winning *Alternative Work Arrangements; Power Up: Transforming Organizations through Shared Leadership*; *Influence without Authority;* and *Influencing Up*. He edited *The Portable MBA in Management*. And his coauthored best-selling text book with Fink, Gadon, and Willits, *Effective Behavior in Organizations*, through its seven editions helped transform the teaching of organizational behavior.

Areas of expertise include leadership and influence, changes in organizations, educational methods, management and organizational behavior, cross-functional teams, family business, management development for international work, negotiations, corporate entrepreneurship, and strategic change. He has served on the boards of several nonprofits, including First Place for Youth, Vinfen, Families for Depression Awareness, and the Cambridge School of Weston.

See web page: www.influence-withoutauthority.com

Pramodita (Dita) Sharma, PhD (University of Calgary), is the Daniel Clark Sanders Chair and professor of Family Business at the Grossman School of Business, University of Vermont. She is a visiting professor at the Kellogg School of Management's Center for Family Enterprises, Northwestern University. She has also been a visiting scholar at Babson College where she served as the academic director of the Global Successful Transgenerational Entrepreneurship Practices (STEP) project for five years. Dita holds honorary doctorates from the Jönköping University in Sweden and the University of Witten/Herdecke in Germany.

Dr. Sharma's research on succession processes, governance, innovation, next-generation commitment, and entrepreneurial leadership in family enterprises has been honored with several international awards. She is amongst the most frequently cited scholars in family business studies. In addition to nine coauthored books, she has published over fifty scholarly articles and book chapters on family business studies. Her book on entrepreneurial family firms (with Hoy) is being used in family business courses around the world and has been translated into Mandarin. And the SAGE Handbook of Family Business (with Melin and Nordqvist) is described as a "must read" and "critical resource for all students and scholars of family business."

Sharma is active in leadership and advisory roles in a number of professional associations. She serves as the editor of *Family Business Review*, a highly ranked journal of business. With Mark Green, she co-founded Family Enterprise Research Conference in 2005. This annual conference attracts leading family business scholars from around the world. In 2013 she launched the Global Family Enterprise Case Competition.

Pramodita received the prestigious Barbara Hollander award at the twenty-fifth anniversary conference of the Family Firm Institute and received the Life Time Influence and Impact award at the 2015 Family Enterprise Research Conference.

Sharma maintains close links with the business community. Supported by various private and government agencies, her research is well received both in academic and practitioner outlets. She is a frequent speaker at gatherings of family business leaders around the world. This interaction enables her to share insights from evidence based research with practitioners while ensuring that her research remains focused on issues of significant importance to the family business community. Experiences and close interactions with her own family's enterprises help keep her professional work rooted into the realties and complex dynamics of these fascinating enterprises that dominate the economic and societal landscape around the world.

Berrett–Koehler
Publishers

Berrett-Koehler is an independent publisher dedicated to an ambitious mission: *connecting people and ideas to create a world that works for all*.

We believe that to truly create a better world, action is needed at all levels—individual, organizational, and societal. At the individual level, our publications help people align their lives with their values and with their aspirations for a better world. At the organizational level, our publications promote progressive leadership and management practices, socially responsible approaches to business, and humane and effective organizations. At the societal level, our publications advance social and economic justice, shared prosperity, sustainability, and new solutions to national and global issues.

A major theme of our publications is "Opening Up New Space." Berrett-Koehler titles challenge conventional thinking, introduce new ideas, and foster positive change. Their common quest is changing the underlying beliefs, mindsets, institutions, and structures that keep generating the same cycles of problems, no matter who our leaders are or what improvement programs we adopt.

We strive to practice what we preach—to operate our publishing company in line with the ideas in our books. At the core of our approach is stewardship, which we define as a deep sense of responsibility to administer the company for the benefit of all of our "stakeholder" groups: authors, customers, employees, investors, service providers, and the communities and environment around us.

We are grateful to the thousands of readers, authors, and other friends of the company who consider themselves to be part of the "BK Community." We hope that you, too, will join us in our mission.

A BK Business Book

This book is part of our BK Business series. BK Business titles pioneer new and progressive leadership and management practices in all types of public, private, and nonprofit organizations. They promote socially responsible approaches to business, innovative organizational change methods, and more humane and effective organizations.

Berrett–Koehler
Publishers

Connecting people and ideas
to create a world that works for all

Dear Reader,

Thank you for picking up this book and joining our worldwide community of Berrett-Koehler readers. We share ideas that bring positive change into people's lives, organizations, and society.

To welcome you, we'd like to offer you a free e-book. You can pick from among twelve of our bestselling books by entering the promotional code **BKP92E** here: http://www.bkconnection.com/welcome.

When you claim your free e-book, we'll also send you a copy of our e-newsletter, the *BK Communiqué*. Although you're free to unsubscribe, there are many benefits to sticking around. In every issue of our newsletter you'll find

- A free e-book
- Tips from famous authors
- Discounts on spotlight titles
- Hilarious insider publishing news
- A chance to win a prize for answering a riddle

Best of all, our readers tell us, "Your newsletter is the only one I actually read." So claim your gift today, and please stay in touch!

Sincerely,

Charlotte Ashlock
Steward of the BK Website

Questions? Comments? Contact me at bkcommunity@bkpub.com.

Certified

Corporation
bcorporation.net